CONSERVATORY GARDENING

■ Creating an Indoor Garden ■

Yvonne Rees & David Palliser

CROWOOD GARDENING GUIDES

First published in 1990 by
The Crowood Press Ltd
Ramsbury, Marlborough
Wiltshire SN8 2HR

This impression 1996

British Library Cataloguing-in-Publication Data

Rees, Yvonne
    Conservatory Gardening
    I. Residences. Garden rooms, Gardening
    I. Title   II. Palliser, David
    635′.0483

ISBN 1 85223 304 4

Grateful thanks to Joan Clifton at Clifton Nurseries for her advice on conservatory plants and kind co-operation with much of the photography; to Susan Heath of Gardens Under Glass; Jeffrey Gold and Richard Mudditt of Town & Country Conservatories for their expertise and information on conservatory structures and interiors; and to all the other conservatory companies who supplied us with details.

Picture credits
Walton Conservatories for Fig. I; Paris Ceramics for Figs 6, 32, 33, 34, 37, and 46; Town and Country Conservatories for Figs 4, 5, 7, 10, 12, 13, 14, 16, 18, 24, 26, 36, 40, and 41; Machin Designs for Figs 2, 8, 17, 29, and 35; Halls Traditional Conservatories for Figs 3 and 44; Room Outside Limited for Figs 9 and 55; Dave Pike for Figs 66, 68, 98, 99, 100, 101, 102, 105, and 106; Gardens under Glass for Figs 25 and 57; Dobies Seeds for Figs 45, 62, 82, and 112; John Brooks (Denmans) for Figs 47, 52, 53, 81, and 114; Martin Summers for Figs 38, 51 and 90; Steve Wooster for Figs 42 and 52 (with thanks to Overbecks), 48, 49, 50, 56, 58, 59, 60, 61, 63, 64, 65, 67, 69, 70, 71, 72, 75, 77, 79, 83, 85, 88, 91, 92, 93, 94, 96, 97, 107, 108, 109, 110, 111, 113, 115, 116, and 117.

All colour artwork by Claire Upsdale-Jones
Typeset by Avonset, Midsomer Norton, Bath
Printed in Hong Kong by the Paramount Printing Group Limited

Contents

Preface

As writers specialising in both interiors and exteriors, from home decoration to garden design, we have been watching the rising popularity of conservatories with interest. The conservatory is the perfect marriage between inside and outside, not simply an excellent link between the garden and the house, but a completely hybrid environment: a fabulous indoor garden where the weather is always fine, plus the bonus of an extra room for relaxing, play, or entertaining, with the magnificent decoration of living plants.

In the first flush of enthusiasm several years ago, all the emphasis seemed to be on the structure itself and both companies and customers would drool over ridge cresting and dentil mouldings, gothic sweeps and arches, and other stylish details borrowed from Victorian and Edwardian architecture. For all the care and cost that went into these elaborate home extensions, the interiors were largely neglected – comprising a few Lloyd Loom chairs, and a couple of tentative house-plants. It seemed a terrible waste when there was all that plant potential to be exploited: the chance to collect unusual, over-sized and exotic species to make a rich display of extravagant foliage and brilliant blooms. For surely this is how the conservatory was intended!

More recently, it has been exciting to see the ever-growing conservatory trend move inside at last, with evidence of far better planned and furnished interiors, a more confident approach to plants and an awakening enthusiasm for exotics. With an ever-increasing number of companies competing fiercely for their slice of the conservatory-grown apple, many are now offering an interior as well as an exterior design service, and there are also specialist companies willing to tackle the task for a fee. For those who prefer to do the design job themselves, the selection of suitable plants in the garden centres and specialist nurseries is improving all the time with new hybrids and new introductions making cultivation and plant care as swift and simple as possible. Thankfully, plants are also starting to be better labelled with details of habit and maintenance – it all helps to encourage greater confidence and promotes a more adventurous attitude towards plants, particularly in the conservatory where tropical and subtropical species tend to be unfamiliar.

A well-stocked and flourishing conservatory, whether it be simply to house your specialist plant collection, or suitably furnished for informal meals and relaxation, can be a real asset to your home and to your lifestyle. We hope, in this book, that you find the inspiration and practical advice to do it justice.

Yvonne Rees and David Palliser
Bryn Hill Cottage, 1989

Introduction

As the conservatory market grows ever larger, encompassing every aspect of these delightful glass extensions reminiscent of a more leisurely age, more and more options are becoming possible. Practical limitations are being overcome and the range of available designs increased to suit every style of home and every size of budget. Modern technology has at last brought the kind of efficiency and sophistication we expect from our homes but which was never achieved when conservatories last had their heyday, towards the end of the nineteenth century.

Today's conservatories can offer all the elegance of the old, or the sleek styling of the new, yet remain energy-efficient and easy to maintain with no leaks or draughts: this is no longer a pleasure to be enjoyed with stoic reservations. Nor does the structure provide the satisfaction of a luxury hard won, guaranteed to rot away without regular maintenance and a

Fig 1 Even the simplest conservatory offers the chance to enjoy an indoor garden at all times of the year, and makes a fine link between indoors and out.

Fig 2 Traditional style, but offering all the opportunities of modern materials: an attractive plant house extension.

significant investment of cash. From the smallest lean-to sun room to the most gothic extravaganza looking like an elaborate wedding cake with its glassy pinnacles, there is a conservatory to suit almost every property and all tastes. Recently, it seems as though a house is undressed without one, its owners deprived of this essential element of modern living. The conservatory is enjoying its role as status symbol again, after a decline almost into extinction. These days, even new houses are being built with conservatories and they are selling five times faster than identical homes without, despite the slightly higher costs.

So what is the great attraction of the glass house extension, or conservatory? Few homes and garden lovers can resist the idea of an all-year indoor garden which can be enjoyed when the weather is too cold to go outside, where one can sit and gaze at the garden through a screen of luxurious foliage and enjoy every minute of sunshine, winter and summer, without a cold wind to take the edge off its warmth. For some, the conservatory still offers an exciting chance to grow more tender plants and interesting exotics. With the addition of heat and controlled humidity the amateur enthusiast can build up a specialist collection of favourites, or devise a magnificent living display of flowers and foliage, incorporating something of interest throughout the year.

Despite the profusion of plants, sometimes reaching jungle proportions in what can approximate a near-perfect atmosphere, the conser-

Fig 3   With the right furniture and accessories, you can create a superb leafy dining room.

vatory is not simply an *en suite* greenhouse. Plants are important, and are prized for being unusual or difficult to cultivate without specialist conditions; but they are arranged and designed as you would plan the garden, different shapes, colours and sizes carefully balanced for contrasts and harmonies, a wonderful mixture of sights and scents with special highlights according to season. It is a display designed to be appreciated at leisure from a comfortable seat nearby – which explains the conservatory's secondary role as a leafy living area, a favourite and stimulating place for relaxing or dining.

The conservatory's interior design must,

therefore, ideally reflect both aspects of its character and use. Floors must be decorative yet sturdy enough and easy to clean to take the kind of mess plants produce; electrical fitments such as lighting must be waterproof, and furniture designed to withstand high humidity and the fading effects of strong sunlight. Hence that unmistakable conservatory atmosphere with its cool stone or tiled floor, airy cane, willow, rattan or cast metal furniture piled with comfortable cushions and, most importantly, the plants, with their oversized, dramatic leaves and bright tropical blooms.

For some, this lush setting is the perfect place

for a swimming pool or a candlelit dinner party. For others, it is the plants which are to be treasured above everything, and they will sacrifice human comfort and the potential of an informal extension to their home by reproducing the hot, steamy conditions of a tropical rainforest for a breathtaking collection of orchids; or by re-creating the cool, damp atmosphere beloved by ferns to develop a special collection. The conservatory is an escape from reality: its surroundings and even its climate are very different from anything else to be experienced within the adjoining home or garden. It is very easy to relax in this little indoor paradise; but it is not a paradise won by accident. That happy profusion of plants is the result of careful planning and a sophisti-cated system of maintenance, much of which can be automated these days.

Get the formula right and the rewards are rich for very little effort, once your conservatory is established. New materials and better efficiency of heating, watering and ventilation systems will ensure you can keep it that way for very little effort and expense – the conservatory enthusiasts of the past would be envious.

THE HISTORY OF CONSERVATORIES

The idea of bringing tender plants inside at night or during the colder months goes back to the

Fig 4 In the tradition of the old-fashioned orangeries, plants can be overwintered in the conservatory and stood outside on the patio in pots during the warmer summer months.

Fig 5   Gothic arches, pinnacles and an elaborate roof design in imitation of the conservatory's rich heritage.

Romans. But conservatories as we know them, with their large areas of glass enclosing an extensive and exciting collection of exotics, has its roots in the seventeenth-century orangeries which were usually built of wood, brick or stone with large leaded windows facing south and a stove or furnace to provide artificial (and rather inefficient) heat within. The orangery was designed as an overwintering facility with citrus trees and other tender fruits brought outside during finer weather to enjoy the fresh air and sunshine in their pots and tubs.

As a wider range of plants was introduced, oleanders, geraniums and myrtles (the 'exotic greens' of the eighteenth century), these elegant buildings had become known as greenhouses or conservatories, that is, a place where plants might be 'conserved'. But it was the passion for tropical plants in the early part of the nineteenth century and the introduction of glass roofs that brought conservatories to their climax. They became architectural wonders of sparkling glass to be built alongside every great house in the country where fashionable fruits such as pine-

9

apples joined the oranges and lemons, and whole permanent displays of dramatic foliage and flowering plants were created.

It did not take long for the craze to spread and for the industrial revolution to put conservatories within the reach of the middle class with their grand town houses and enthusiasm for current trends. Improved technology meant better glass manufacture and the development of cast iron to replace the old timber structures, with the chance to create elaborate arches and curves. The architects loved it. The intrepid explorers of the nineteenth century were sending back an ever greater selection of fascinating plants to be nurtured, demanding bigger and more elaborate conservatory space. People flocked to the great glasshouses open to the public: the Palm House at Kew, or Crystal Palace, built for the Great Exhibition in 1851, and tried to reproduce the effect at home. The conservatory at Chatsworth, built about a decade before, was already famous, home to wonderful palms and ferns as well as bananas and superb tropical water lilies.

Under the enthusiastic care of the indefatigable Victorians, lush arrangements of tropical and subtropical plants flourished; massed beds were filled with a rich profusion of different foliage plants to create the impression of a tropical jungle. Special conservatories were designed and maintained, thanks to improved heating systems that no longer gave off poisonous fumes, to ripen off peaches, apricots and nectarines for the table or coax tender species to flourish. Those who could afford it specialised. There were special cool ferneries, vine houses and collections of rare plants, often displayed in an imaginative setting that included artificial grottoes, fountains and sculptures.

By the time conservatories had moved into the Edwardian era, they had become even more elaborate and heavily accessorised. The late nineteenth century had already seen a swing in

Fig 6 (opposite) A Victorian-style interior is easy to reproduce with old-fashioned floor tiles and dramatic foliage plants, as in this simple unheated lean-to.

popularity towards more temperate plants and the newly developed, less delicate cultivars of tender exotics, which allowed a more comfortable environment where their owners could spend their leisure time sitting amongst them, enjoying them at closer quarters and maybe sharing the experience by entertaining a few friends. Here were rampant climbers, flowering shrubs and hardy herbaceous plants, lofty palms and all kinds of foliage plants densely arrayed in pots or on shelves, in contrast to the old planting beds with their formal arrangement of paths in between for interesting perambulations. By now the conservatory was fully furnished with tiled or mosaic floors, oriental rugs and the wicker furniture we still identify with conservatories today.

In this wholly familiar format, conservatory style crystallised, and remained popular for some thirty years, perhaps encapsulating those relaxed, golden afternoons spent among sweet-smelling, lush plants before the First World War shattered the illusion. Few could allow themselves the luxury of heating and maintaining a glasshouse full of exotics, however, and tender plants soon died without warmth and regular attention. The structures themselves began to decay and fall apart, a very small percentage surviving to be restored in later years by a few discerning enthusiasts – but not until well after the Second World War.

Technology has since moved on again to offer attractive, affordable modular units which, thanks to mass production, improved glass techniques and electronic controls or sensors to reduce maintenance to a minimum, are as practical as they are lovely. Even the structure is manufactured to last, with little or no care. In the closing decades of the twentieth century, the conservatory has reached a new climax of interest, reflected in a revival of exotic and unusual plants in the nurseries and garden centres, and improved availability of conservatory-style furniture and accessories. Its timing is exactly right, meeting a modern eagerness to create ever more living space, and the search for a relaxing and pleasant escape from stressful lifestyles.

CHAPTER 1

Choosing Your Conservatory

Having decided you would like a conservatory of your own, you may be wondering what it is going to involve and where to start. Preparation and construction is quite an upheaval and even the simplest, smallest conservatories are not cheap once you take into account the necessary accessories, cost of plants and furnishings. A more ambitious structure will represent quite a considerable investment, one you will not want to waste by choosing badly. It is important to be aware of all the practical implications of owning a conservatory before you commit yourself too

Fig 7 A charming conservatory neatly taking up hardly any room at all, on a town patio.

Fig 8 Your conservatory will be geared to your style of home, to your budget and how you intend to use it. Here it opens on to patio and pool area.

deeply or set your heart on a particular dream.

Building regulation approval may be required for a conservatory, although those covering an area of less than 30sq m/108sq yds are not normally liable in the UK. The same is true of planning permission, which is generally only necessary on structures exceeding 70cu m/824cu yds. Properties sited in a national park, facing a public highway or historically listed may need official approval and you should check with your local planning officer. Many conservatory companies are prepared to handle this side of the job for you, checking whatever permission is required, organising site preparation and contracting building work right up to finished construction, and should be able to advise you accordingly.

When it comes down to choosing exactly which conservatory is going to be right for you and where you are going to put it, there are three limiting factors: the space you have available, the way you intend to use your conservatory, and how much money you have to spend. Obviously, one closely influences the other: if the only available space is limited or faces north, this will limit its use; budget is often the dividing line between an off-the-peg, lean-to conservatory and one specially designed and fitted to match the shape, size and style of your home; while if you are determined to use the conservatory as a living area all year round, you should be looking at conservatories that can offer the option of double glazing and an efficient heating system.

Fig 9   This well-planted, multi-purpose living area with its practical yet decorative furniture is the perfect link between house and garden.

The most sensible and satisfying approach seems to be to start with the ideal, your dream conservatory; then to explore the practical considerations and modify your plans accordingly. Try to look logically at why you want a conservatory, how you would like to use it and in what way it will affect the nature of your house. Like any other home extension, it is maybe a good idea to completely rethink the other rooms in the house to see how a conservatory could improve your general living quarters.

Often it makes good sense to switch some rooms around. For example, the focus of attention has changed in many older houses and rooms designed to serve a certain role are used in a very different way today. The emphasis has changed from the front to the rear of the house; instead of wanting to create an impressive front to the world, these days we prefer privacy and quiet for our living rooms, a place where we can relax and enjoy immediate access to the rear garden. This is why we now see an increasing number of kitchens sited in the front of the house, in rooms that were once considered far too grand for such a purpose. A conservatory is frequently used to provide extra living space and to ease the burden on the rest of the house, which enables those rooms to be redefined. It can also provide a valuable link between house and garden, the latter becoming increasingly important as an area of relaxation.

The extent to which your conservatory is going to take over the role of another room will determine the fabric and design of the structure – and the part plants will be able to play in it. Your main kitchen, dining room or sitting room may encompass a conservatory atmosphere with lots of glass and a carefully selected display of plants, but it cannot truly be considered a conservatory, an environment where conditions would not be suitable for fine furniture or food preparation. However, as an occasional dining area for a sunny early-morning breakfast or exotic dinner parties with friends, an informal sitting room where you can escape for a good read or a sundowner, wicker furniture or ranges designed for garden

Fig 10   A few pieces of furniture, a rug and a couple of ornaments can convert the conservatory into a delightful living area, especially if you keep it simple as with this stunning pink and white theme.

use and a few carefully chosen accessories, will combine comfort and good looks yet are perfectly practical, and indeed look highly appropriate, in a leafy environment.

Most popular current use for a dual purpose plant/people conservatory is as a dining area. This is partly due to the revival of interest in entertaining friends at home and in preparing more elaborate family meals. Also, the dining room tends to have been squeezed out of our homes in recent years, forced to share space with the kitchen or living room and losing its identity for special occasions. Provision for dining in the conservatory is an exciting prospect amongst dramatic plants and sparkling glass; the effect is even more dramatic at night when a centrally situated table is perfectly reflected in the roof above and lamps or candles can be used to highlight specimen plants or create romantic reflections in the glass. This type of conservatory needs good insulation and efficient heating at night, plus a good selection of night-scented or evening-blooming plants.

15

Conservatories also make superb living areas and a few comfortable chairs, an occasional table, and maybe a rug or two are all that is needed to create a delightful leafy retreat to which all the family will want to escape at every possible opportunity. Whether or not you install the luxuries of heating and lighting will depend on the extra cost against how often you will want to use the room. An east-facing conservatory may be just your 'morning room', making the most of early sunshine; alternatively, a west-facing one may encourage you to linger from early evening onwards. That feeling of seclusion and privacy also suggests the use of the conservatory as a home office or hobby room. Here a sturdy table or work top, a telephone point, power points and spotlights make it possible to concentrate away from the rest of the house in a delightful atmosphere. You might even be able to incorporate shelves or trollies for books and papers if your chosen plant display does not require high levels of humidity.

Another popular use of the conservatory as a dual function room is the indoor pool house or leisure room. With its jungle atmosphere and views of the garden, it is perhaps the perfect setting for an indoor swimming pool, and a large conservatory is an obvious and popular choice. It need not adjoin the house – some are linked by means of glass covered corridors or walkways so that you do not have to go outside to reach the pool. If you haven't the space or the money for a full-sized swimming pool, the much smaller but equally fun hot tubs and spas take up very little room and fit neatly into the most modest of conservatories, still leaving room for an exciting display of exotic plants. Such specialist use demands certain practical conditions to be satisfied if it is to be a success. Plants must be well contained and kept away from the pool or spa so that soil and dead material cannot pollute the water. Nor does the chemical cocktail in the pool, absolutely necessary for human hygiene, do much good for your plants, and they can be damaged if splashed or soaked. You will also have to plan for a specialist air conditioning system to cope with the excess condensation under such circumstances; these can be linked to your heating system and recycled to help reduce heating costs; there are specialist indoor pool companies who can advise on the equipment available to handle this.

If you are hoping your conservatory will serve more as a major extension to the home and you want to incorporate a kitchen or other major functional room – a conservatory bathroom is not unknown, especially in second-storey structures – your plants will have to take secondary importance and the conservatory itself be adapted accordingly to suit your more stringent needs. Facilities for necessary services such as water, gas, electricity, extra drainage and ventilation, better insulation, sturdier basic construction and so on, will also have to be provided.

SIZE AND LOCATION

We tend to be jealous of garden space, yet we want to maximise and extend our living area. The conservatory is a good compromise and unlike a bricked and roofed home extension, you won't begrudge giving it plenty of room, even where the garden is small. Generally, it is worth going for the largest conservatory you can afford to build and maintain; this gives you maximum space for plants and, should you wish it, for furniture and other trappings of a living area. As a general rule on practical dimensions, one square foot of glazing can maintain four square feet of floor space, based on a temperature of around 19–21°C/66–70°F, taking into consideration the likely amount of heat generated and lost by day and night. Satisfy these requirements and the garden is your oyster. The shape of your house and the size of space available will often suggest the most suitable dimensions for your conservatory, and the space within will be adjusted to suit.

When choosing exactly where your conservatory will go, the most obvious place is not always the best one. There may be several

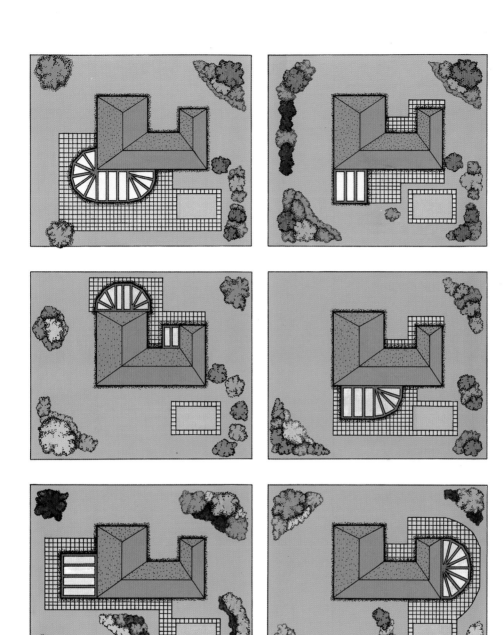

Fig 11   Even buying a ready-made conservatory from one of the modular component ranges results in a wide choice of options and positions. You should plan the final site carefully in relation to both house and garden layout, and bearing in mind areas of maximum sunshine and shade. This detached home with large garden and swimming-pool shows some of the possible options using the shape of the building and paved patio ideas to link house and conservatory to the pool area for practical and enjoyable use.

Fig 12   Care should be taken to orientate the building correctly so that it enjoys the right amount of light and warm sunshine. Here a site between the two wings of the house was ideal.

Fig 13   Space can be found for a conservatory almost anywhere, as this grand entrance tucked into a corner goes to show.

options and you should think carefully about that most important question – where does the sun come from? When considering likely positions, make sure you know which way your house is orientated, whether facing north, south, east or west, as this will affect the performance and possible plant content of your conservatory.

A south-facing conservatory may sound ideal, capturing the hottest sun for the longest period. However, solar efficiency is such that it can get a bit too hot, and unless you are planning a cacti house or a specialist plant conservatory for a similar plant group that prefers hot, dry conditions, a south-facing structure can be too arid and scorching for both plant and human occupants, if there is no system of shading and ventilation. Much better is to install a west- or east-facing conservatory that will receive a more measured dose of sunshine, with high points in the morning or evening accordingly. A north-facing conservatory may sound like a pointless exercise, but in fact, although heat and light levels are reduced, you will receive a good, steady source of light and cool conditions suitable for some plant groups such as ferns and ivies, which will not tolerate the warmer atmosphere of the average conservatory.

To find the best site, explore all the possibilities. The conservatory does not have to be at the rear of the house but could run along the side or even be at the front, if this provides better orientation. Sometimes the best solution is to position your conservatory away from the house altogether; it is better to have perfect conditions a short walk away, than a disappointment and a room you barely use attached to the house.

Where space is really limited, the solutions can be quite ingenious, especially in towns and cities. The conservatory may only be large enough to span a former side passage; or create a pleasant porch or entrance, yet it still offers the opportunity to grow an interesting selection of plants, with maybe room for a couple of chairs and a table so you can sit and enjoy the sunshine too. Nor does the conservatory have to be at ground

Fig 14   If a conservatory adjoining the house is impossible or unsuitable, consider a free-standing structure at the opposite end of the garden, which may be better orientated.

level. It may fit neatly on top of a single-storey, flat-roofed extension, or be used to glass in a terrace or balcony, while a roof-top conservatory is often magnificent, with excellent views and the chance to enjoy a sheltered garden under what are usually cold, exposed conditions. If you still can't find the space for even a small conservatory, it may be possible to replace the roof of an existing room with an ornamental glazed conservatory roof, which will still add sufficient feeling of light, space and warmth to produce an authentic conservatory atmosphere.

There are other factors that influence the perfect site for a conservatory. Ideally, shelter from cold winds is advisable since their chilling effect can result in higher heating costs. You may have to plant a windbreak of trees or install screening to block a bad draught, providing this is not close enough to cast too much shade. For the same reason, take care that existing trees and fences are not too close; nearby trees can be an added nuisance by dropping leaves, branches and fruits on to your glass roof. At ground level, watch out for manhole and inspection covers which may have to be altered; you cannot build over drains and access covers without consulting your local authority. You will also have to make allowance for any pipework, chimneys and windows on the main house which might be obstructed by the conservatory structure;

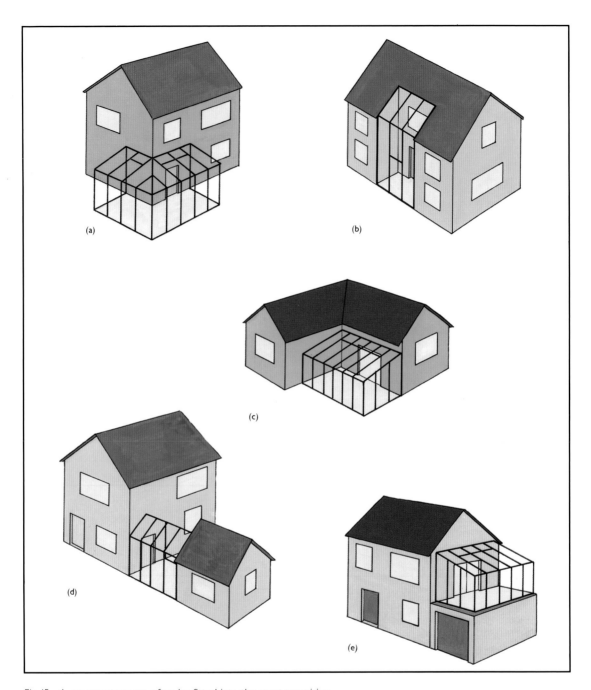

Fig 15 A conservatory can often be fitted into the most surprising places, especially with town houses where available space may be limited. (a) A corner-designed conservatory makes the most of two aspects and maximises the amount of interior space. (b) The conservatory can often be used to fill in an awkward space or to link several rooms with a central living area. (c) Lean-tos are economical and can be fitted to one or two house walls depending on the convenience of your house design. (d) Conservatories can be used to link to buildings. (e) A roof-top or first-floor conservatory is sometimes the only option.

Fig 16 This conservatory has been neatly built opening on to a first-storey balcony, and is linked to the garden by a series of steps framed by elegant wrought iron work.

however, these are minor problems which can usually be overcome by means of linking units or a valley construction, so it is never worth siting the conservatory in an inferior position because of them.

SHAPES AND STYLES

One of the reasons why conservatories have become so popular is that everyone likes the way they look: being mostly made of glass, and with an ethereal quality, they seem to suit any style of building, their traditional shape at once elegant and ornamental. If you think about it, the same size and shape extension in brick and slate would look awful in most instances. A huge choice of architectural styles and configurations is available, including more modern designs with large picture windows, and softly curved rather than gothically angled profiles. However, the basic most popular style remains the same, from the very plain and simple lean-to conservatory, to the glorious glass palaces with their arched roofs and fine detailing. Architecturally, conservatories have changed little since their era of popularity in Victorian and Edwardian times, and the more elaborate types are copies from those periods.

21

Fig 17   Modern design can incorporate pleasing curves in the basic structure; this is frequently seen in new lean-to designs.

Aiming to suit the style of your home as closely as possible, most conservatories incorporate a brick, stone-faced or timber base to match the house construction, usually continued to a height of 45–90cm/18–36in. Brick or stone is the better choice if you are going to build planting beds inside, as timber is more likely to rot. If you are planning raised beds, the wall should come to the level of the top of the beds for neatness. Some

lean-to models are glazed right down to the ground, to create the illusion that the conservatory continues into the garden, especially if you match pots and paving. The main structure is available in a choice of timber, painted white or left natural, or in aluminium alloy finished in white, silver or bronze. White, natural western red cedar, or red pine timber finish are the most popular for traditional-style conservatories.

Fig 18   A brick base can help link conservatory to main building, especially if you can get hold of matching old brick, as here.

Conservatories can be purchased in a choice of three basic formats. They can be simple and inexpensive, a ready-made sun room which can be installed with the minimum of fuss, more of a glazed lean-to facility. It is not ornate or highly attractive and will not support sophisticated heating, ventilation or shading systems; but it does provide the opportunity to grow a few more tender plants and, skilfully positioned, has good heat efficiency and will enjoy the full effect of the sun when it shines. The lean-to looks best against a long wall, but can also be positioned in the corner between two walls, although this limits its effectiveness. Where no suitable wall exists, it is possible to build one and simply link the structure to the house at one end. More ornamental conservatory designs are also available off-the-peg, and if chosen and sited carefully they can look attractive for moderate cost. Styles are becoming more sophisticated all the time, with various decorative optional extras; but generally these tend to be the simpler styles and it will depend on the design of your house and space available whether they suit.

For greater flexibility of design, many manufacturers are now offering their conservatories as component parts, a standard but extensive range of modular units which allows you to create exactly the shape and size structure to suit your needs and the practical limitations of the site. Ranges may be adaptable enough to provide an almost unlimited number of configurations. Simpler, but less flexible, complete, self-contained units which may be linked together are offered by some companies: they may be hexagonal or octagonally shaped to provide scope for attractive 'honeycomb' designs. Most suppliers offer advice and suggestions on how component parts can be put together to make suitable conservatory designs.

Top of the range are the custom-made conservatories, designed exclusively to match the architectural style of your home and expertly built to your own specification as well as that of the space available. This is the option for those with the money to spare and who are looking for a conservatory that is unique. It is also often the only choice for homes with difficult requirements such as limited or awkward available space, beyond the scope of any of the component part ranges. The specialist knowledge and advice such companies can offer also makes the tailor-made conservatory the best solution for upper-storey constructions, also link and rooftop locations, with their rather special practical requirements.

When comparing ranges and choosing a suitable manufacturer, you should check exactly what you are getting for the price. Some companies can offer a complete service from researching local building regulations to planning the position of the last plant; others can only supply the structure and you will have to arrange for the preparation and building work to be done yourself. This will involve the digging of foundations, usually to the same depth as those of the house, the installation of footings and a proper

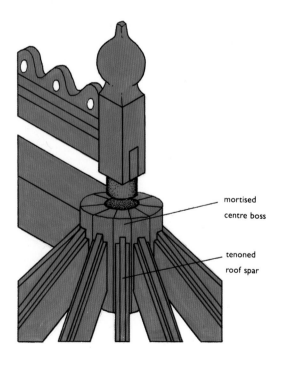

mortised
centre boss

tenoned
roof spar

Fig 19 Detail of roof structure.

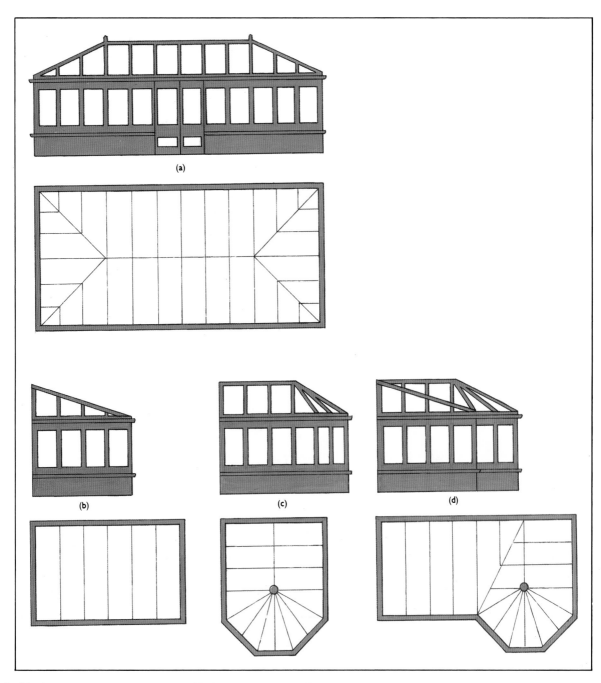

Fig 20   Standard conservatory designs.   (a) Central ridge design, front
elevation and floor plan.   (b) Lean-to/rectangular, side elevation and plan.
(c) Octagonal design, side elevation and plan.   (d) Lean-to/octagonal, side
elevation and plan.

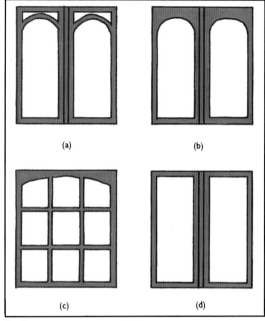

Fig 21   Window designs.   (a) Sweep arch-top windows.   (b) Solid arch-top windows.   (c) Georgian arch-top windows.   (d) Plain windows.

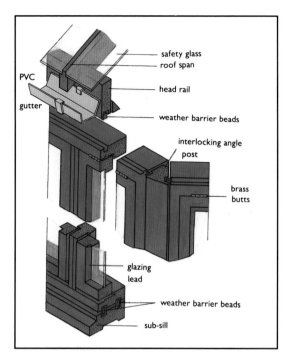

Fig 22   Double glazing systems.

drainage system, not too close to the foundations. The majority of conservatories require a 10cm/4in layer of hardcore covered by a concrete slab, then a damp-proof membrane, and a cement and sand top screed. Some manufacturers can supply a prefabricated base at extra cost.

It is important to establish whether or not the price you are quoted includes erection of the conservatory and the glazing – with the less expensive conservatory ranges, this could increase the basic cost by nearly 50 per cent. Many of the less expensive ready-made ranges come in kit form to be erected yourself, or by a local builder. Then there are the other facilities, many of which could be considered essential, such as shading and ventilation facilities, including automatic systems, secure doors, plus brass door and window furniture, all of which are frequently optional extras.

Double glazing is another extra cost which many consider well worth it for the better energy efficiency it offers (up to 50 per cent of heat loss), especially at night when temperatures can drop dramatically. With double glazing you can increase personal comfort and save on heating costs – an important consideration where the conservatory is going to be used as a room throughout the year. However, for older properties needing sympathetic style and atmosphere, the double glazed option is not always satisfactory for aesthetic reasons – practically, the glazing bar has to be thick enough to cover the glue and while the traditional ⅝in Georgian-style bar sometimes works, it never looks as good as the original slender profile of period windows. Also optional is toughened or wire-reinforced safety glass for the roof, another option worth the extra cost if there are many trees nearby or if you get a lot of snow in your area.

Additional costs might include attractive decorative details such as ridge cresting,

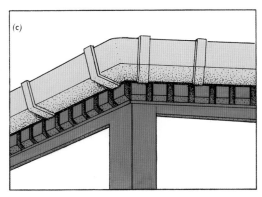

Fig 23 Decorative details. (a) Victorian sweeps will visually soften the architectural lines of the structure and have a distinctly gothic air. (b) Ridge cresting along the apex is a fine decorative addition if you are looking for an old-fashioned-style conservatory. (c) Dentil mouldings are a classic touch offered by many manufacturers.

ornamental mouldings and other 'curly bits' that will give your conservatory an authentic traditional flavour and a real touch of elegance. Some companies extend their service further to offer, for an appropriate fee, a complete interior planning and installation service from floors and staging to the plants and furniture themselves. Their advice and the easy availability of necessary items this provides may be welcome to those lacking in experience or who are unsure of what to buy.

OUTSIDE LANDSCAPING

We have talked a lot about making sure the conservatory looks good and in keeping with the house; but it is equally important for it to relate to your garden too. The perfect way to link conservatory to garden seems to be to build a patio or terrace immediately beyond the conservatory door. This not only provides an excellent visual link, especially if paving material is chosen to suit that of the interior, it also reduces the amount of garden dirt and debris being brought indoors. Tubs and containers placed on the patio can also be selected to match those inside the conservatory. Or play visual tricks with indoor and outdoor pools.

When landscaping the rest of the garden, remember to incorporate the conservatory as a decorative feature, which the more ornate models certainly deserve. Take the time to view it from various possible angles within the site to provide the best focal points and maybe offering

Fig 24   Where the building opens out on to a patio, furniture and plant containers can be chosen to match.

glimpses through shrubs, trees or screens; or present it as a focal point from the other end of the garden. You should also think seriously about the kind of views you are creating to be seen through the conservatory windows by day – and spectacularly by night – if you intend to install garden lighting. You should always bear in mind that nothing tall should be sited close to the conservatory, where it might create unwanted shade or obscure a fine view.

CHAPTER 2

The Right Environment

Before you can make a decision on essential fixtures and fittings (many of which will be offered as options within your conservatory package), you will have to be clear in your mind as to exactly the kind of environment you are hoping to create. If you have read the previous chapter, you will have had some thoughts on the subject already and your inclinations will have influenced size, shape and position of the structure, as has been discussed.

Now is the time to settle positively on whether the conservatory will be functioning primarily as plant house or as living room. Is its humidity and temperature to be geared to

Fig 25   Planting has been kept strictly under control with a massed arrangement of different foliage shapes in this stylish black and white interior.

human comfort or that of a specific and hard-to-please plant group such as ferns or orchids? Selecting the correct facilities from the outset will ensure a successful and easy-to-maintain conservatory that will provide all the enjoyment you anticipate. Get the details wrong at this stage and you are sure to be disappointed and beset by problems such as plant failure, too cold or too hot conditions, or the spoiling of furniture, flooring and other fittings.

HEATING

To maintain the required temperature in the conservatory, you will have to shade the glass during periods of strong sunshine during the day and provide some form of heating at night and during the winter. Your decision to heat the conservatory may be ruled by cost rather than the plants you would like to grow or the number of days you would wish to spend in it.

A completely unheated conservatory is still a sun trap in summer and on sunny days in winter, although in a north-facing structure the strength of the sun is diminished. You could still create a splendid display of hardy plants such as palms, conifers or interesting foliage plants like bamboos, or *Fatsia japonica* with its large, glossy hand-shaped leaves, to which spring bulbs and summer annuals in pots would add seasonal colour. The room will become very cold overnight and during the winter, so plants should be chosen carefully for their hardiness. Remember also that you are limiting your own use of the area and that the unheated conservatory can only provide a seasonal sitting room or dining room.

Maintaining a maximum winter temperature of 4.5–10°C/40–50°F still won't produce conditions warm enough for you to relax in, but it will extend your range of plant possibilities to include a wide number of more tender mediterranean plants, many of which can tolerate certain extremes and enjoy a level of humidity that is still comfortable for humans. The upper limits of this

temperature scale will make a noticeable difference to your fuel bills. With these kinds of temperatures, the air should be kept dry until the weather begins to warm up in spring, when you should start increasing humidity levels in proportion to the rising temperature.

If the conservatory is your chance to grow the tropical and subtropical exotics you have always loved, temperatures will have to be considerably higher, especially during winter, with high humidity to match. These steamy conditions are unlikely to be considered comfortable enough for the conservatory to be used as a dining or sitting room, so this range of plants demands a plant house conservatory – and substantial heating costs. The alternative, if you are anxious to enjoy the best of both worlds, is to section off an area of the main conservatory with glazed screens – a bay would be ideal – to create a small orchid house or whatever, with its own specialised atmosphere. This would also keep the area separate from pets and children, enabling you to build up a collection including possibly poisonous and delicate plants. If this is not practical, you can still incorporate a few slightly tender species in your collection by selecting more tolerant cultivars, and possibly overwintering them in the house providing you can approximate the required warmth and light – on a living room window sill perhaps. Special plant lights (*see* page 78) may be necessary to compensate for short winter days in the house: rooms may have the heat, but not the conservatory's potential for capturing all available natural light.

As a general rule, there should be a 5°C drop in temperature overnight in the heated conservatory in order that plants photosynthesise correctly. As the heat is needed more at night than during the day (when the sun will supply surprisingly high levels), your source of heat will need to be carefully planned, especially as these requirements are usually the direct opposite of your domestic needs.

It pays to over-estimate the capacity required so that you have the extra on hand for extreme cold conditions should they occur; it would be a

Fig 26 More of an elegant sitting room than a plant house, this fine conservatory with elevated views of the garden is fully heated and features old-fashioned radiators that look perfectly in style.

shame to lose your more tender species through an unprecedented severe cold spell. It may be necessary to install an independent system or incorporate a sophisticated thermostatic control when running the heat off your main supply. As a beneficial side-effect, you can be reassured that the conservatory will act as a wonderful solar unit in respect of whatever room it adjoins, keeping it surprisingly warm and permitting the room's heating to be turned down low.

The most economical method of heating a conservatory is to link it to your existing domestic system. However, this will rely on whether it has sufficient spare capacity to supply the temperatures you need. If this is not possible, an independent system is needed. It brings its own advantages in that it can be programmed to supply exactly the rise and fall of heat you want at any required time. A separate circuit is certainly the best option if you are serious about your plants and if night-time temperatures in particular have to be strictly controlled. While the conservatory is still at preconstruction stage, it may be worth considering underfloor heating, which neatly resolves the problem of where to site radiators, especially in a small conservatory,

31

and provides an excellent, steady all-over heat source with no hot spots or draughty corners. This means less condensation and better humidity control. These advantages relate only to the hot water underfloor installations which, once they are heated up, act like a giant storage heater and can be run from any kind of fuelled boiler from solid fuel and oil to mains and bottled gas. The kind that heats the floor by rneans of electric wiring is not recommended since it tends to be expensive to run and not very efficient.

An excellent alternative for the conservatory is trench heating, which also uses water pipes and flush cast iron gratings so you still save on floor space; or if you are not worried about aesthetics (or can think of a way to dress them as a decorative feature), hot water pipes can be run round the walls to provide a fairly dry heat. Either of these systems, or standard radiators – the traditional short, cast-iron type looks most in keeping in the conservatory – can be run from a choice of fuels. Boilers can be sited outside the conservatory and run on your personal choice of fuel: even solid fuel can offer a sophisticated range of automatic controls these days, and these are well worth taking advantage of if you are keen for your conservatory to virtually run itself.

The alternative to central heating is free-standing or independent heaters, which may be the best option for a small conservatory looking for its own, inexpensive to install system, or a top-up heat source. Stalwart of the greenhouse is the paraffin heater which is efficient at keeping the conservatory frost-free, but not for maintaining consistently high temperatures. Some models include thermostatic controls and all are reasonably cheap to run. The 'blue flame' type produces less plant-toxic fumes, but all produce rather a lot of water vapour and require regular attention, which makes them unsuitable if you are looking for easy-to-maintain facilities. Free-standing bottle gas heaters offer similar problems, although they require far less attention and maintenance. They are portable and efficient but produce a tremendous amount of water vapour, which can cause condensation problems.

Electric heaters produce a reliable dry heat, need no maintenance and can be fully automated. Their drawback is that they can be expensive to run, although thermostatic controls and the chance to take advantage of economy periods for night-running may make this a competitive choice. There are many types of electric heaters, including: convection heaters, useful for large conservatories; tubular space heaters, which can be fastened to the sides of the conservatory and are fairly unobtrusive; oil-filled electric radiators which offer all the neatness and convenience of a centrally heated system; hot air blowers or fan heaters which provide quick, efficient heat (and new models incorporate frost-guard facilities that mean they come on automatically when the temperature drops below a certain level). However, fan heaters can be irritatingly noisy and must not be positioned where they can blow directly on to plants.

VENTILATION

Good ventilation is essential to reduce the temperature in summer, when the magnified effect of the sunshine can make the conservatory unbearably hot and stuffy (bright sunshine can quickly bring temperatures up to 38°C/100°F, even in winter). It is also vital because plants require a certain amount of fresh air to flourish. You must have roof lights as well as side lights;

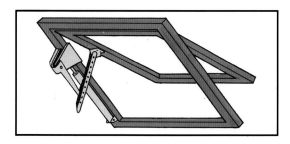

Fig 27   The best form of ventilation operates automatically via temperature-sensitive hinged vents or windows. These can be adjusted to open at any temperature.

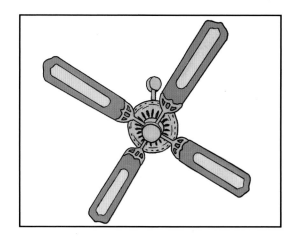

Fig 28 A classic colonial-style fan is a stylish
way to keep the conservatory a little cooler.
Some units incorporate lighting too. For your
own comfort, reversing the fan will add a little
warmth to the conservatory on colder days.

opening the doors on to the garden in summer can also be a valuable way of introducing and circulating more fresh air. Vents and louvres should be easy to control, and an automatic system is preferable. A point worth noting is that it is the first 10cm/4in of opening that provides the desired effect, so they need not be opened any further than this, as long as you have enough of them. This way you can provide adequate fresh air without creating a security risk or allowing rain to get into the conservatory.

Electric fans are also useful for cooling and freshening the air, but again these can be noisy. Fans are usually mounted in or near the roof and may be of the extractor type, or they may be circulating fans which control the temperature of the air by the speed at which they move it round. Some of the more decorative styles give a decidedly colonial air to a furnished conservatory and can even incorporate lights within the unit.

LIGHT

As discussed in Chapter I, the position of your conservatory (whether it faces north and thus has good light but lower temperatures, or south, capturing maximum heat and light) influences natural light levels. However, if you will be using your conservatory at night as a place to entertain friends or to sit and relax, you will need to consider artificial lighting. Special plant lighting designed to influence growth patterns, and spotlights hidden among foliage to create dramatic effects are discussed on pages 78–79.

Ambient lighting should be equally subtle and carefully planned to create the right effect. Try not to limit your ideas to domestic-style lighting, although a central chandelier can work splendidly in the right setting. Hanging lanterns look good because they are soft and decorative, unlike spotlights which tend to bounce reflections off the glass. The exception is small, low-voltage spotlights which are directional and can be used to highlight a particular plant or area, such as the dining table. For atmospheric dinner parties, candlelight can be spectacular – or try Victorian glass nightlights which provide softly flickering reflections. Remember that all your lighting effects will be reproduced in the glass overhead, resulting in an exciting night-time interior if you get it right. For a dramatic and eye-catching vista from the conservatory, you could also light up the garden using outdoor lamps and spotlights to highlight plants, fountains and other features.

SHADE

One of the biggest problems in conservatories is not how to keep them warm enough for tender plants, but how to cool down the effects of magnified sunshine. Since it is harder to cool a room than to heat it, preventative measures are necessary, in the shape of shades or blinds. It is an area perhaps not satisfactorily resolved in conservatory design, but there are various options. In a south-facing conservatory the problem may be so acute that you should perhaps consider breaking up the roof area so as not to have too large an area of glass.

The ideal solution to overheating is outside

Fig 29 Shade is essential for most plants, particularly the majority of foliage species. Narrow slats in natural materials both filter light and look highly attractive.

screens, but as yet there does not seem to be a perfect, permanent system. Fixed Venetian blinds do the job, but do not look very attractive; the alternative is old-fashioned cedar slats, which are heavy and do not roll up very well and so are best left in position. They can be mounted on raised runners so that they do not interfere with ventilators and can go right down to ground level if required. This system is extremely efficient and looks lovely from the inside, the 2.5cm/I in-wide lathes producing a wonderful stripy light. However, they look rather an eyesore from outside and many people find them unacceptable if their conservatory structure has been particularly chosen for its elegance and architectural good looks.

Internal blinds may be rattan, plastic-slatted or, not highly attractive but functional, plasticated fabric punctuated with small holes; you could use wood, reed, netting or polythene sheeting, all effective for shading plants modestly without cutting out a tremendous amount of heat. You can also buy laminated glass incorporating a ceramic stripe, which helps cut the glare but obviously reduces light in winter as well as summer.

Automatic winding systems ensure that screens and blinds are raised and lowered as re-quired, employing an electronic thermostat and light sensors. You can also buy non-retractable aluminium louvre blinds which can be fitted internally or externally and used to control the level of light within. Fitted internally, the louvres will filter the light efficiently, allowing a certain level of light through for plants even when fully closed; fitted outside, they will help control both light and heat.

FLOORING

The floor in the conservatory needs to be tough and hard-wearing, waterproof and easy to clean. If the area is going to be semi-furnished for human occupation, you will want it to be decorative too. A surface that can take a good hosing down is ideal as this helps maintain humidity levels in summer and it is a good idea to incorporate a drain in the floor when you are laying the concrete subfloor.

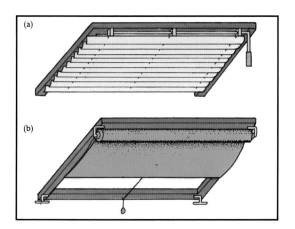

Fig 30 Shading systems. (a) Roller-slatted blinds fitted above the roof are the most efficient means of shading. (b) Interior blinds help reduce light but do not significantly alter excess heat levels.

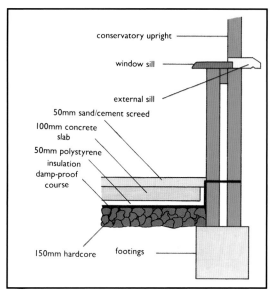

Fig 31 Incorporating a layer of insulation between floor and ground will retain heat gained during the day and transform the concrete slab into a simple form of night-storage heater.

35

Fig 32 *A strong design or bordered pattern is ideal in the conservatory, and decorative ceramics take hard wear.*

Fig 33 *A tough, hard-wearing floor like these antique tiles is essential if floors are to be hosed down regularly to improve humidity, and to cope with the inevitable plant debris.*

Fig 34 *Unglazed decorated floor tiles give the conservatory a traditional style.*

If your conservatory is designed for plant use only, you may be content to leave a floor with its final concrete screed, given a couple of coats of sealant to make it easier to clean. More attractive would be some form of garden paving or, if you can guarantee the conservatory will be frost-free, plain quarry tiles. The plant conservatory that doubles as stylish sitting room or dining area requires more thought and design flair. Despite the stringent practical requirements, there is a wide range of options, not just among garden paving but also within certain specialist interior flooring ranges such as quarry tiles, where you will find many different earth shades, shapes and sizes, making it possible to create interesting patterns with squares and hexagons, maybe using black quarry tiles for contrast or decorative ceramic inserts between them. Ceramic tiles themselves offer an almost unlimited choice of patterns, colours and designs which can really exploit the shape and style of the structure from mural pictures to tessellated contrasting colours

36

Fig 35   This wonderfully relaxing living area was created using the sturdiest of furnishings; wicker furniture, rugs and cushions are all good companions for leafy green foliage plants.

(black and white is a traditional favourite) to strong mediterranean patterns and mosaics. Like quarry tiles, they are as tough as they are good-looking and, with the right grout, are completely waterproof. It is important to use tiles recom-mended for flooring use, as these are slightly thicker and have been fired at higher tempera-tures for better durability.

Natural stone tiles also look good on a con-servatory floor, creating a pleasing visual link

37

Fig 36 Here is a well-planned and welcoming interior that is as practical as it is comfortable and pleasing to the eye. Hardwearing timber floor laid in traditional herringbone design incorporates neat heating grilles; basket furniture is just right in both style and suitability.

between inside and out. These might be old flagstones, honey-coloured York stone or steely grey slate, all of which can again be laid in decorative patterns and borders, yet will last for centuries. Brick also makes an attractive conservatory floor and again comes in a choice of natural colours. For added interest, lay them in herringbone or basket-weave patterns, or create a central, circular design to echo the circular shape of your conservatory design. For a really stylish conservatory, you can buy marble tiles which look very luxurious combined with lots of leafy plants and the occasional elegant statue. Marble paving must have a slip-resistant surface for safety.

If you want to soften areas, near seating or dining furniture for example, use rugs which can be taken up and cleaned should they get dirty, or removed in order to hose down the floor. A fitted carpet is certainly not suitable, even those recommended for kitchen or bathroom use, if you are planning a proper plant display – nor do

they suit the purpose and appearance of the conservatory. Go instead for rush or coir matting which is tough and attractive, with a very natural appearance; for real luxury and comfort, oriental-style rugs and dhurries can look superb on a hard flooring with rattan or cane furniture and exotic plants. Care should be taken not to get rugs wet or badly soiled.

FACILITIES FOR PLANTS

With plants taking pride of place in the conservatory, their needs must be considered before other more decorative facilities. We have already discussed practical requirements such as heat, shade, water, fresh air and light, but you must also consider how you are going to display your plants and where you are going to plant them. The type of collection you are aiming at will control these choices to a large extent. For example, a collection of one plant type, and therefore a reduced range of plant sizes, will require stag-

Fig 37 A massed arrangement of different foliage shapes creates an exciting jungle effect, even if it is only a few pots pushed together.

Fig 38 Specially fitted shelving like this is useful for displaying a wide selection of smaller plants.

gered shelving or staging to maintain an interesting display at different levels. *In situ* plant beds encourage a natural, dense display of plant specimens and are useful if you are hoping to create a leafy jungle effect. The beds could be raised and more formally planted with textural foliage plants, scented species or brightly coloured flowers for disabled conservatory users. Plants are often simply put in position in tubs and containers, themselves highly decorative and, best of all, portable so that they can be moved around according to plant needs or removed altogether according to season.

Staging

Plant staging can be as simple as a single bench, or tiered in order to build up a three-dimensional display of smaller pot plants. It generally comprises hardwood or aluminium components which fit together to form supports and shelves according to your needs. Wrought iron styles are also available should you want a more decorative effect. Staging is easily dismantled and reassembled should your needs change. The material for the staging should be selected to suit the main structures of your conservatory.

Staging is highly suited to automatic watering systems using trays of sand or capillary matting. Stepped shelving or staging certainly makes most efficient use of space and provides lower shelf areas for plants that prefer a slightly shadier location. Staging is normally arranged around the sides of the conservatory, keeping the centre clear for furniture. However, in the large conservatory you may like to divide the floor area with a free-standing display of plants. You can also buy shelving specially designed to fasten to the roof area for trailing or cascading plants.

Planting Beds

You should try to incorporate some direct planting beds in your conservatory, particularly if you are hoping to grow shrubs and climbers or other large plants since they will grow more efficiently and the soil will not dry out so quickly. Ideally the beds should go right through to the soil at floor level, but a lot of people seem reluctant to install them for fear they are going to be messy and difficult to keep under control. You might like to consider raised beds built to a height of around 30–38cm/12–15in and which are useful for raising plants up a little without spoiling the view out, and which can be edged in timber, stone or tiles. Fill with a mixture of two-thirds loam, one-third peat, as most plants prefer an acid-based compost. Direct beds should be well dug and enriched with plenty of organic material such as well rotted manure or garden compost. It is a good idea to mulch the surface between plants with bark chips, pebbles or gravel which helps slow down the evaporation of moisture, discourages weeds and looks very attractive, especially while plants are growing to fill the gaps.

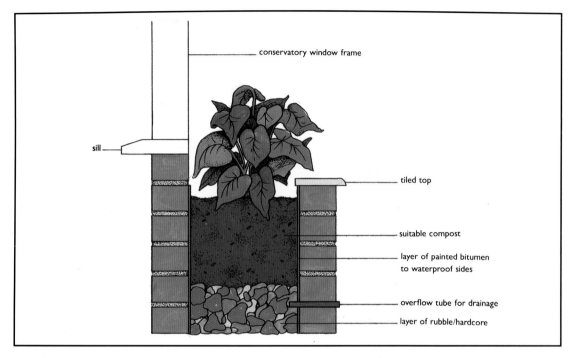

conservatory window frame

sill

tiled top

suitable compost

layer of painted bitumen
to waterproof sides

overflow tube for drainage

layer of rubble/hardcore

Fig 39   If your conservatory has a brick or other type of solid base you can incorporate planting beds, which offer more scope for permanent plant displays and climbers like jasmine and bougainvillea, giving more room for their roots.

Pots and Containers

The wide range of pots and containers available serves to extend the decorative scope of your conservatory interior. Providing you select the correct size and fill it with the appropriate compost (*see* page 95), the choice is up to personal taste and the kind of atmosphere you are hoping to create. Glazed Chinese ginger jars encourage an oriental look; plain and decorated terracotta pots always seem to have a Mediterranean air about them. These special ornamental containers are ideal for large specimen plants in prime position as the focal point of your conservatory display. For the large number of pots ranged on shelves and staging, ordinary flower pots will suffice. Choose between clay and plastic: plastic pots are light and easy to clean but despite plenty of drainage holes in the bottom, they are

not porous like clay. This can be a disadvantage when plants are at risk of being waterlogged, or should you wish to consider an automatic watering system. Both plastic and clay pots come in a range of standard sizes from very small to those large enough to take small trees or shrubs. There are also containers designed for specialist use, such as half pots for shallow rooted plants and orchid pots which have holes in the sides.

Some orchids must be grown in special slatted baskets which must be hung up to allow the flowers to bloom from below. These make an

Fig 40 (opposite)   Your choice of plant containers can range from weathered garden terracotta to elegant glazed oriental pots in blue and white ceramic. This jungle arrangement of dark green foliage shapes uses a successful mixture of styles, with the occasional hanging basket to add extra height.

attractive eye-level display. Hanging baskets for other plants, such as bright annual flowers or ferny foliage plants, can look good but they are difficult to water and the compost dries out very quickly. More successful perhaps, and very attractive, are big wicker baskets suspended from the roof and lined with fibreglass and four layers of polythene. Unless you are prepared to spend the time watering twice a day and keeping plants in prime condition with regular grooming and attention, it is perhaps advisable to keep hanging baskets to a minimum or to plant them up with a display of geraniums or something

equally sturdy. Baskets may also be made from wire, plastic or clay and should be firmly attached to your conservatory's roof or side-structures, so do check regularly that hooks and chains are sound. Similar containers are available for fastening to the wall or side-structures.

On the floor and bench, you may like to pop your pot inside a more decorative container, which usually does not have any form of drainage and completely hides the more functional plant pot. These might be specially designed cache-pots made of glazed pottery and highly decorated with exotic patterns, floral or relief

Fig 41   Mass plants together on shelves or in troughs and use individual tubs or containers for special flowering effects at different times of the year.

designs. Alternatively find your own original containers amongst household basketware, glass, china, wood — even metal such as old copper kettles or preserving pans. There is no end of objects that make attractive containers from kitchen ware to antique chamber pots. If the container is non-porous, you can pack the space between it and the plant pot with damp peat or moss to improve moisture retention, a useful device for damp-loving plants such as ferns. If you are not placing your pot inside a non-porous decorative container, it should be provided with a dish or saucer for taking excess water and any soil that may be washed out of the drainage holes.

Much of the charm of a conservatory plant display lies in the close proximity of different plant types. Pots can be simply grouped together on a shelf or tray at least 8cm/3in deep, which means you can position them closer together. Even more effective is to arrange the pots in a deep trough which hides the pots, or to plant them directly into the container. Troughs come in many shapes and sizes, are made of stone, wood, pottery, plastic and metal, and may be designed to sit on a shelf or window sill, or be free-standing on their own legs. If placing the pots directly into the container, layer it with damp gravel to encourage a humid microclimate amongst the closely positioned plants. Peat packed in the spaces between the pots also encourages a damp atmosphere. These plants will subsequently require less water than free-standing plants and you should be careful not to overwater — lift out the plants occasionally to check that water is not standing in the bottom.

To plant your group directly in the container, choose species with similar needs but a good contrast of shapes and colours. The container must have drainage holes and be filled with a good, free-draining planting mixture. Leave sufficient space between plants to allow for growth; a top dressing of pebbles or chippings between the plants looks decorative and helps maintain moisture until plants have spread a bit. If you suspect one of your plants is sickly, or if one

specimen is out-growing the others, allow the trough to dry out a little then tip the contents out gently to examine the roots for any damage. Prune and tidy up, removing any dead material, and replacing diseased plants with new ones as necessary.

Plant Supports

Climbing plants, whether self-climbers or creepers requiring training, need some form of support. The simplest method for the conservatory with its large expanse of glass is a system of horizontal wires at 20–30cm/8–12in intervals along the back wall and sides of the structure.

Heavy gauge galvanised or plastic-coated wire can be secured by means of special fittings for

Fig 42 Climbers can be trained over timber or plastic-coated trellis, here painted white to match the back wall. Note the excellent variety of heights, shapes and colours within the foliage.

metal frame or eye-hook screws for a timber-framed conservatory. When using wall nails to secure wires to a back wall, make sure the wires are supported slightly away from the wall to allow air circulation behind the plants. In some conservatories, wooden or plastic-coated trellises may be possible, supported by means of special brackets.

Indoor Pool

An indoor pool can look delightful even in quite a small conservatory, and it is surprisingly easy to construct. It makes an excellent focal point and provides the chance to grow exotic looking water plants, whilst also improving humidity levels. The pool can be sunk, or raised and edged in brick, stone or tiles to match your flooring.

A sunken pool will have to be excavated at construction stage and incorporate a ledge about 20cm/8in wide below the level of the water if you wish to grow dramatic marginal plants like rush and iris. The pool can be lined with butyl rubber or a preformed fibreglass pool liner, which comes in a wide range of ready-made shapes and sizes. Disguise the edges by overlapping your flooring material, or make a natural arrangement of rocks and boulders for a more informal look.

A raised pool is built in approximately the same way, only the liner is enclosed within the raised structure and lends itself to more formal styles such as regular geometric shapes. The pool could be no more than a few inches high; or large and deep, with a wide, formal stone slab coping that doubles as a seat for observing plants and fish. If you would like to grow water lilies or to keep fish in your pool, it must be at least 45cm/18in deep.

An informal pool will often fit neatly into the corner of the conservatory; in a large one, it might be more extensive, crossed by bridges and stepping stones as it meanders through a display of exotic plants. The formal pool, based on a single or linked design of geometric shapes, makes an excellent focal point in the centre of the conservatory. Alternatively; borrow a clever oriental idea and butt it up to the conservatory wall of glass with an identical pool installed immediately on the other side in the garden, like a mirror image. This not only creates a clever visual illusion and links inside to outside, but the Japanese like to make the pool continuous, running right under the foundations so that precious Koi carp, bred for their wonderful markings, can swim freely between the two and take refuge in the warmer indoor pool when the weather is cold.

If you can, try to incorporate a moving water feature in your indoor water garden plans, as this will increase humidity and improve the oxygen of the water. The addition of a submersible electric pump run from a low voltage electric supply (many kits come complete with transformer) means you can incorporate a fountain, water spout or even a waterfall cascading from a pile of rock in an informal jungle-style conservatory. Even if you have no room for a pool, a water pump will enable you to design and fit miniature moving water features that take up very little space, but which still add that delightful sparkle and sound of running or trickling water, with the benefit of greater humidity of course. Water might be allowed to trickle or pour from a wall-mounted stone head or simple spout into a bowl or basin, be incorporated into a free-standing fountain or large urn filled with water and planted with the smallest water-loving plants, or converted into a 'bubble fountain' where the water simply bubbles up like a spring between a pile of boulders or pebbles, being recycled in a concealed reservoir beneath. The only real disadvantage of a fountain or water spout is that you will not be able to grow water lilies in the same pool, as they prefer calm water.

FACILITIES FOR PEOPLE

For most of us the conservatory is not just an excellent opportunity to grow an indoor collection of exotic plants, it also provides a useful and rather lovely extension to the home. Providing it

Fig 43   Conservatory furniture.   (a) Based on an original Victorian design, this cast metal furniture is highly ornate and will last for years. Slatted seats add comfort.   (b) Decorative plant stands and pots can be used to accessorise the living area.   (c) A traditional curved-back seat in cast metal is a pretty addition to a small conservatory.   (d) Willow furniture is light but strong and easy to maintain. It is available in natural finish or can be spray-painted in a wide range of seating options.

Fig 44   This brand new conservatory is ready for planting with low perimeter shelving for pots and containers of foliage plants and the occasional hanging basket to add interest at eye level. Fresh flowers could be used to add highlights.

is sensibly furnished, it can certainly add a valuable asset to your living facilities and provide space to relax or entertain friends. However, it is important to realise at this stage that because of its dual nature and the rather inflexible demands plants make on the environment, the area is only really suited to being used as an informal sitting room or sunny breakfast room, a spectacular leafy dining room for special dinner parties, or perhaps to use as a home office.

Conservatory Furniture

Unfortunately many people fail to realise that ordinary living room and dining furniture is not suited to the conservatory. This is not simply because the style looks out of place, but also because expensive upholstery and polished timbers are easily damaged and soiled in the damp, sometimes extremely hot, bright atmosphere. Printed fabrics will also fade in the strong sunshine unless specially treated – those used on conservatory furniture are designed to be fadeproof. Instead, try traditional colonial-style rattan or cane furniture, which looks very good sur-

rounded by jungle-type plants and natural materials – it is a good compromise between indoor and outdoor furniture. Generally speaking, any kind of furniture designed for the garden is also suitable, and it is worth looking out for some of the more attractive ranges for your conservatory interior. If you are trying to recreate a Victorian-style atmosphere you can buy cast aluminium chairs, tables and love seats imitating the old traditional cast iron furniture, usually painted white and highly decorative, featuring fruits, flowers and figures.

Some of the timber ranges are very smart too, in a choice of hardwoods and including a wide range of chairs, tables and benches for lounging or dining. The addition of pretty cushions would be a welcome and decorative soft touch without making the furniture impractical for conservatory use. If it is comfort you are looking for and you will be treating the conservatory more as a kind of indoor garden or sun room, attractive modern plastic-coated aluminium loungers and chairs are readily available. Some styles will fold away for convenient storage should yours be a warm weather-only conservatory.

CHAPTER 3

The Plants

The conservatory is primarily designed for plants – a giant glass showcase, maximising available natural light and heat, which provides the perfect opportunity to control the plant's environment with artificial heat and ventilation (*see* Chapter 4). It offers every houseowner with the space to spare, a chance to grow the more tender but interesting varieties of plants with confidence. It allows the gardener to experiment with exotic tropical and subtropical species, or the amateur specialist to indulge in a collection of different cacti, orchids, ferns or other difficult-to-please plants.

Such scope and opportunities are an exciting prospect, both for the keen plantsperson and for the interior designer looking for a stimulating leafy environment to serve as sitting room, sun room or mock alfresco dining room. Huge architectural foliage plants and brilliantly coloured blooms can supply as many creative design

Fig 45 You can rely on a collection of cyclamen for a bold display of exotic seasonal colour. This is a hybrid mix of hot pinks against white blooms and deep green marked foliage, called Firmament Mixed.

Fig 46 The success of a jungle-like display relies on a good contrast of shapes and heights, but subtle variations in plant shades. Taller plants and climbers maintain interest and eye contact right up to the roof in this well-planted interior.

Fig 47 The delicate butterfly blooms of a tiny cyclamen in a stony arrangement of strange-shaped succulents.

Fig 48 This display gives some idea of the richness that can be achieved with a patchwork of different plants and a limited colour scheme, using staging and shelving to vary the height and position of plants.

possibilities as the most comprehensive range of furnishing fabrics and decorative wallpapers. How sad, then, that so many of today's conservatories, beautifully designed and architecturally inspiring, with stylish furniture and smart floors, are so poorly furnished when it comes to the plants. Whether from laziness or lack of confidence, specimens are frequently restricted to a token handful of familiar house plants, the kind that tolerate a good deal of neglect and which are often left to fend for themselves – the ubiquitous spider plant, *Chlorophytum*, a weeping fig, *Ficus benjamina*, or perhaps a sturdy *Tradescantia* or two. Quite apart from the lack of imagination and waste of potential this represents, plants chosen without proper consideration of their needs and position are unlikely to flourish. The last two like plenty of light and moderate warmth but will reward your lack of concern by shrivelling up in strong sunlight.

That wonderful jungle atmosphere or balanced display full of interest you've admired in the best conservatories is not a lucky accident or a matter of putting a few chance plants together. To look that good, the arrangement must be carefully planned, individual species chosen for compatibility and selected to provide a good, balanced range of foliage contrasts, blending different shapes, sizes and shades. Points of special interest need particular care so as not to overdo or dilute the effect of seasonal highlights like tubs of flowering bulbs in spring, a summer-flowering shrub or climber, or plants designed to peak in autumn or winter. The selection should ideally provide something of interest throughout the year, not a riotous display that is over in a month or two.

Thought should be given to colour also – not all combinations are complementary, and subtle blends of creams and yellows, blues and mauves, pinks and silvers, or deliberate eye-catching contrasts of strong red, blue or purple highlighted by gold or white blooms, are far more successful than a strident juxtaposition of mismatching pinks or reds (notoriously difficult shades to combine well). Remember that foliage plants contribute their own colours and patterns to your living conservatory patchwork, and your back-

49

Fig 49   *Red adds a note of drama to your scheme but should be used carefully as a highlight or special display, like this cascade of blooms, to avoid overdoing the effect.*

Fig 50   *Staging within the conservatory will enable you to display a large number of plants with minimum maintenance.*

ground planting could make or break the overall scheme. Make them work to your advantage by offsetting brilliantly coloured blooms with dark, glossy evergreens or a subtle blend of different greens; highlight more subdued areas with silver- or grey-tinged varieties, or cream, silver, gold and white variegated forms, which have interesting spots, stripes and splashes.

Single specimen plants, strategically positioned to complement furniture and furnishings, may look fine in the rest of the house, but the conservatory is for massed arrangements, a leafy screen like a living curtain which softly filters the bright sunshine through those large areas of glass. Apart from the visual advantages, plants grown together will create their own mini ecosystem and be naturally inclined to thrive, seeming to enjoy the company. However, this arrangement will only be truly successful if you take the time and trouble to choose species that prefer the same growing conditions (light, heat and humidity), so that you can provide approximately

the environment they need, as described in Chapter 2.

Conscientious maintenance is important, for an enclosed, artificially controlled environment like the conservatory, with large areas of glass which encourage high temperatures and poor ventilation, is the perfect breeding ground for pests and diseases. You must be diligent about watering, spraying and shading your plant collection according to their specific requirements, and provide correct ventilation.

It also helps to keep the area clean and tidy, by removing dead or diseased blooms and foliage, clearing spilled compost immediately and keeping beds and containers topped up or well mulched. It not only maintains a pleasant, smart environment for lounging or dining in (if that is the intended purpose of your conservatory extension), but also keeps plants healthy. A healthy plant is a strong, lively specimen and makes your display all the more attractive. Also, a regular check means problems are more likely to be spotted early when a mild remedy can often

Fig 51 (Above)   A rich collection of leaves and
flowers with a red and green theme, arranged in
pots on staggered shelves to vary the height and
breadth of this display. The plants seem to rise
out of a carpet of tiny leaved, green Helxine.

Fig 52 (Below)   Many succulents are rosette-
forming and need careful watering. They look
particularly effective grown together as a
group of strangely varied fleshy shapes.

Fig 53 *Succulents love hot, dry conditions and will produce a wonderful variety of exotic shapes and forms in greens, greys, blues and mauves.*

avoid more drastic, time-consuming and maybe expensive action.

It is a good idea to familiarise yourself with the routine maintenance necessary to run a ship-shape conservatory and, before you start buying any plants, make sure you are aware of the implications and commitment involved with your chosen species. Some are a lot more demanding than others, and gearing your final selection to the time and trouble you are prepared to spend on them later will help to avoid the miserable sight of a conservatory full of sickly or neglected specimens. Being honest with yourself at the outset will result in a much happier relationship between you and your plants.

Householders with busy lifestyles or a hectic family life would be wise to choose a flourishing background of sturdy foliage plants, content to tolerate wide-ranging conditions and minimum care, highlighted by the occasional spectacular but reliable flowering cultivar to provide seasonal diversions. Those with more time to spare or a keen interest in a particular plant group will seize the opportunity to create the ideal environment for a collection of exotics or their own special favourites, which are often easy enough to cultivate but demand quite specific conditions.

PLANNING A PLANT COLLECTION

A great many of your familiar house plants will thrive in the conservatory, growing to twice the several useful design principles that will help narrow down your choice, as well as the practical limitations already mentioned.

The secret of success is to plan the plants in your conservatory as carefully as you might design a furnished interior. In many instances, this is not a bad analogy, for where the conservatory is destined for use as an extra sitting room or atmospheric environment for stylish dinner parties, the plants will be serving the same ornamental purpose as paint or paper, pictures, prints or other decorations; that large expanse of floor-to-ceiling glass is like any blank wall.

Close attention to height and scale are essential in the conservatory and since plants are going to be the primary form of decoration, there is plenty of room to indulge yourself in the luxury of flamboyant flowering climbers or plants with oversized, dramatic foliage. It is a common mistake to think too small and restrict your ideas no higher than eye level, waist level even. You will need to attract attention towards the roof structure, that soaring architectural fantasy of glass and girders which is the focal point of most conservatory designs. Climbing plants are ideal, when trained to follow the basic structure of the building, and they soften it with attractive foliage and showy flowers.

There is an excellent selection to choose from for both cool and heated conservatories, from pretty *Thunbergia* with its mass of cheery yellow and orange flowers to the exotic bell-shaped blooms of the Chilean bell flower *Lapageria rosea*. Larger shrubs and trees are also useful for supplying high-level interest, and tender species will do very well in tubs and containers providing they are kept well fed and watered. Popular for creating an elegant, sophisticated setting are ornamental mediterranean trees like bay and citrus, grown as standards which, when clipped to shape on a single, tall stem, look very attractive in a tub or formal wooden Versailles planter. These can be stood outside on a sunny patio during the warmer months, to be returned to the conservatory display in winter.

Also useful for adding height to your arrange-

Fig 54 Citrus trees can be overwintered in the conservatory where they make a fine specimen plant with their fresh green foliage and bright fruits.

size. However, few enjoy direct sunlight and most like good humidity, so it will be necessary to provide adequate shade and to spray them regularly, maybe twice a day in summer. On the other hand, it would be a shame to limit your collection to the 'old favourites' when the frost-free environment of even a north-facing, unheated conservatory offers the chance to grow more tender varieties of shrubs, trees and climbers. A little artificial heat throws the field wide open, allowing you to grow a wonderful range of exotics. In fact the choice is so extensive and exciting that making an initial plant selection can be a little daunting for the amateur. In recognition of this, some conservatory companies and garden centres offer a complete plant planning service – but if you prefer to take up the challenge yourself (and it can be great fun researching and selecting exactly the right plant for a particular position) or you wish to build up a collection slowly as your interest develops and budget permits, there are

Fig 55   You should aim to add height to your scheme by using hanging baskets of trailing plants, or training climbers to cover the roof along wires.

ment are hanging baskets filled with ferns (in cool conservatories), creeping and trailing foliage plants or bright summer flowers like begonias and fuchsias. Some orchids demand to be displayed in this manner, since their blooms grow out of the compost at the bottom of the plant and have to be grown in special slatted planters. Hanging baskets looks good (*see* page 93 to find out how to prepare them properly), but they are not altogether successful or practical under conservatory conditions – with the compost or moss exposed on all sides it tends to dry out too quickly and plants are also at risk from the effects of strong sunlight above. Thorough watering means lifting down heavy containers and soaking them in buckets of water until the compost is saturated; using a can or spray is never wholly satisfactory and can be most inconvenient if furniture and furnishings are positioned below.

To achieve a pleasing, three-dimensional plant display, you need to plan a good variety of different plant heights and sizes within the total scheme. This involves a little guesswork in the early stages in order to assess the speed at which a particular plant will reach an expected height and spread. This is less of a problem where your plants are in containers, since these can be moved around as and when required to maintain the best effect; you will find creeping plants useful for filling in gaps, especially the more vigorous, fast-growing varieties where a temporary, leafy effect is desired. Generally, taller plants are positioned to the rear and heights should be graduated towards the front, bearing in mind that natural light will be filtered by the foliage. Turn this factor to advantage by selecting those plants which prefer not to be in direct sunlight for the front of your arrangement. The same effect

Fig 56 *Small citrus trees and shrubs will do well in the conservatory, and may even fruit profusely. This specimen has the added advantage of attractive variegated foliage.*

Fig 57 *The conservatory need not be large but it can be highly decorative, even in a limited location like this tiny town backyard.*

could be achieved without resorting to the large specimen plants, by positioning smaller species on staggered staging or shelving at different heights (a treatment often necessary when planning a single plant type display).

Within this well-planned and skilfully balanced arrangement, you should also aim for a good variety of shapes, colours and textures, creating contrasts and harmonies between foliage, flowers, fruits and other plant features. The exciting scope available makes the possibilities endless for both cool and heated conservatories – leaves may be large and leathery, small and soft as velvet, or finely feathered like the bristling plumes of the exotic Sago Palm (*Cycads*) or, for cool, shady corners, the curious Tree Fern, *Dicksonia antarctica*. Blooms might be large and waxy, deeply ribbed like the extraordinary inverted trumpets of the winter-flowering *Datura sanguinea*, or a mass of tiny star shapes like

Christmas tree lights along the plant stems. There are spiky shapes, soft rounded leaves and petals, heart shapes, frills and indentations, tendrils, spikes and tongues, large arrow shapes, thick, fleshy foliage, blooms reminiscent of insects or shiny saucers – all make excellent design material for your conservatory display. There is a kaleidoscopic range of colours at your fingertips too; the flowers can be almost luminous in their brilliance, but foliage can also offer every shade of green, grey, gold, silver, purple, white and cream, as well as variegated forms incorporating coloured stripes and borders, spots, splashes and bands – sufficient choice to be the envy of any interior designer. Add to your scheme something of special interest at high points throughout the year, for example a spring-flowering shrub or winter-blooming orchid. Make sure that you choose only plants that enjoy a similar range of conditions, and you will be guaranteed a successful and enduring display through the year.

55

Fig 58 Codiaeum variegatum.

EFFECTIVE FOLIAGE

Traditionally, the Victorian conservatory maintained a magnificent jungle of exotic palms and ferns, a dramatic backdrop of splendid foliage shapes and extravagantly sized plant forms. This satisfied the nation's love of over-stuffed interiors and their fascination for anything new and unusual (regularly sent home by the shipload from intrepid explorers of the time). In the large, public glasshouses and conservatories like Kew and Crystal Palace, plants could take on the fantastic dimensions of giant palms, curious prehistoric-like tree ferns or the spectacular *Victoria* lily, so large that a child could picnic on its huge, flat leathery lilypads.

In our own modest way, we are trying to reproduce that lush, rich effect in today's conservatories, a large number of which are designed and built in the Victorian and Edwardian architectural style. These days we have access to a far greater variety of imported exotics and tender species, perfect for displaying in the protected environment of the conservatory. Sophisticated hybrid forms can offer a wider range of sizes and colours, combining the best attributes of a particular species by creating plants that are quicker and easier to cultivate, resistant to disease, more reliable and often more beautiful. Such a wide choice is reassuring but essential; as foliage plants are going to form the background planting of your conservatory scheme, you will be looking to maintain a good balance of different leaf types, and your final selection will have to be ideally adapted to your chosen conservatory environment, be that cool and shady or hot and sultry. With a strong framework of evergreen, leafy plants, maintenance is reduced to a well-oiled routine, relying on a few strategically positioned and carefully chosen flowering plants plus the seasonal addition of specially planted tubs and containers of short-lived blooms to provide extra interest through the year.

When looking for interesting plant shapes and striking contrasts, palms and ferns seem perfect candidates, instantly capturing a 'Victorian parlour' atmosphere. However, most prefer cool, moist conditions, while the majority of modern conservatories seek the sun and a hot, dry environment. The more tolerant types may do well in a shady part of the room or close to an indoor pool or fountain where humidity levels are better, but generally speaking, their lovely frondy and feathery forms are only really practical in a very cool, probably north-facing conservatory (see Special Collections, page 65).

There remains, however, a great many plants to choose from, some with fern- or palm-like foliage, others with leaves shaped like hearts and arrows, swords and tongues, huge leaves and tiny ones, soft furry textured foliage and big bold shiny evergreens. A selection of different shapes and forms will automatically produce that rich jungle effect of exciting contrasts and varying light patterns through the patchwork of leaves.

If it's palm-like plants you are looking for and your conservatory tends to heat up in summer, consider the butterfly palm, *Chrysalidocarpus lutescens*, one of the elegant palm-like *Dracaena* or a frondy *Howeia*, which will tolerate warm conditions but must be kept well shaded. *Rhapis excelsa* prefers cool conditions and grows to around 1.2–2m/4–6ft, with palmate foliage arranged on top of long, tough stems.

Introduce some contrasting shapes such as the grass-like False Aralia, *Dizygotheca elegantissima*, a rosette-forming Bromeliad like one of the gaily coloured *Neoregelias* or maybe the small,

Fig 59 Hydrangea macrophylla *(top).*
Hydrangea *'Lacecap' (bottom).*

rounded leaves of *Fittonia*, a low grower useful for the front of your plant display. Some excellent foliage plants can offer the bonus of attractive flowers as well as finely shaped leaves – *Episcia cupreata* with its soft red and silver foliage and tiny red flowers perfect for hanging baskets or disguising the edge of containers, is a good example and you will find many more among the recommended flowering plants on pages 106 to 110.

Showy flowers can be almost superfluous, with the spectacular range of foliage colours which are available for conservatories. With shades ranging from reds and purples to greys and blues plus all the variegated options of silver, gold, white and cream, individual varieties need positioning carefully to avoid unhappy colour combinations where two strong shades are put too close together. The best plan is to restrict your planting scheme to different shades of green from mere green tinged cream to deepest, darkest glossy evergreen and use the deeper and lighter colours judiciously to add highlights or dramatic contrasts. Some species can offer some quite remarkable colour options from the coppery young foliage of the Coffee Plant, *Coffea arabica* (a pretty, multi-purpose plant with its fragrant white flowers and red berries which ripen into the familiar coffee beans), to the purple Velvet Plant, *Gynura aurantiaca*, whose hairy leaves are long and pointed, to the soft grey foliage of the olive, *Olea europae*. There are also the startling variegated combinations of the green and silver Chinese Evergreen, *Aglaonema crispum*, the popular red, green, cream and pink *Caladium* with its large arrow-shaped leaves, or the tongue-like Cabbage Palm, *Cordyline terminalis*, particularly stunning in its 'Tricolor' form which combines shades of pink, cream and green. The Screw Pine, *Pandanus*, offers a range of options for clever colour blending, including pale green striped with white, dark green with yellow stripes and dark green with red spines.

CLEVER CLIMBERS

At least one climbing or twining plant is essential in the well-planned conservatory, supported on wires or a wooden trellis to provide high-level interest and soften the effect of the structure. There is not only a large and excellent selection to choose from for both cool and heated conservatories, here also is a group of plants that offers one of the finest combinations of interesting foliage and superb flowers you could hope to find to suit such specialist conditions. Many are quick growing and vigorous, enjoying plenty of light but grateful for some shade from the direct sunlight overhead; they serve an extra useful purpose in filtering the light for plants below.

The cool conservatory is at no disadvantage when looking for exotic blooms and handsome foliage. Coral Vine, *Antigon leptopus*, is a perennial climber with arrow-shaped leaves and

Fig 60   Dracaena deremensis *'Warnecke'.*

pretty pink flowers which likes plenty of humidity, as does *Hoya*, an evergreen producing delicate clusters of star-shaped flowers. For a real touch of exotica, you should be able to grow Morning Glory, *Ipomoea*, that will quickly smother a wide area with trumpet-like purple flowers; or the hardiest Passion Flower, *Passiflora caerulea*, with its familiar but extraordinary sci-fi blue blooms. The Gloriosa Lily, *Gloriosa rothschildiana*, is equally stunning with deep pink blooms; or for strangeness you would be hard to find a plant to beat the odd-looking red and purple bells of the vine *Rhodochiton volubile*.

Not quite so showy for their individual blooms, but highly attractive in their own way, producing a curtain of massed, small flowers, are the fast growing and always popular Jasmine, *Jasminum polyanthum*, justly loved for its fine, feathery foliage and the bewitching fragrance of its tiny white flowers in winter. Another alternative is Black-Eyed Susan, *Thunbergia*, with bright black-spotted orange flowers. Less often seen but equally attractive and well worth con-

Fig 61 Philodendron *'Imperial Green'.*

sidering are the summer scented flowers of the Chilean Jasmine, *Mandevilla suaveolens*, which also has handsome heart-shaped leaves; while for autumn you might like to enjoy the beautiful red waxy bells of the twining plant *Lapageria rosea*. A popular evergreen with pretty soft blue flowers for a cooler look is leadwort, *Plumbago*, which flourishes in cool to moderate temperatures and is a sub-tropical climbing shrub; it is best supported by canes or wires.

The exotic shapes and eye-catching colours of fine flowers are all very well, but where you simply want your climber to provide good leafy cover, take your pick from the glossy green Kangaroo Vine, *Cissus antarctica*, a strong climber; the fast-growing Cup and Saucer Vine, *Cobaea scandens* (which is a useful annual for fill-

ing a space quickly and does actually produce highly attractive flowers, but not until late in the season); or the more delicate foliage of an *Asparagus falcatus*, a twining evergreen, and the feathery *Asparagus myriocladis*. The obvious climbing foliage choices, vines and ivies, are not always ideal since they do not do well in warm conditions – the conservatory needs to be very cool for them to flourish. Turn instead to tough *Philodendron* for an excellent selection of glossy foliage plants that will make a fine display, providing they are given good humidity in spring and summer; choose from green- or copper-coloured forms or heart-shaped *P. scandens*.

There is no shortage of choice of climbers for the heated conservatory either, and most of these tropical or sub-tropical species produce breathtaking or interesting blooms as a bonus to some fine foliage. Herald's Trumpet, *Beaumontia grandiflora*, is well named with its white trumpet blooms and large oval leaves. Golden Trumpet, *Allamanda cathartica* 'Grandiflora', is maybe even lovelier, the large yellow flowers as much as 8cm/3in across.

Introduce exotic scents with *Wattakaka sinensis*, whose fragrant white flowers have red spots against grey foliage; or *Trachelospermum asiaticum*, a sun-loving evergreen whose white and yellow flowers are also scented. Some of the more tender passion flowers could be grown under warmer conditions: hybrids with even more extraordinary flowers and remarkable colour combinations of purple, red, white and pink. There are other climbing plants whose flowers are so curious, they will create a real talking point in the conservatory: Parrot's Bill, *Clianthus puniceus*, is maybe one of the most familiar but no less strange, the flower clusters spiked scarlet like exotic insects against feathery foliage. The Flame Pea, *Chorizema cordatum*, produces its orange and yellow flowers against a background of spiny heart-shaped leaves; the Coral Pea, *Hardenbergia monophylla*, makes a veritable curtain of mauve and yellow flowers, and *Cestrum purpureum* has clusters of hanging burgundy blooms. The Purple Bell Vine, *Rhodochiton atrosanguineum*, is an irresistible combination of heart-shaped leaves and odd-looking bell-like red blooms with dark purple pronounced 'clappers', a real curiosity for the warm conservatory even if the plant itself is short-lived.

FLOWERS FOR SCENT AND COLOUR

Flowers are the highlight of your conservatory planting scheme; they add new shapes and colours to your basic framework of evergreens and climbers, and some can also contribute the added delight of a heady fragrance. Ideally you should plan for something to be in bloom

Fig 62 The Winter Cherry, Solanum, *is a compact leafy green plant smothered in glossy fruits, a useful splash of colour when not much else is blooming.*

through most of the year and this should be possible in the cool or heated conservatory if you choose your plants carefully and position them where they will have most impact. However, it is the heated conservatory that offers most scope for year-round interest, for if you can maintain certain levels of heat through the colder months, you can take advantage of some of the winter-blooming exotics such as shrubs and orchids. Specially planted tubs and pots of forced or early varieties can, of course, be introduced into any type of conservatory as soon as the plants start to come into flower and left in place until the blooms start to die back, at which point they can be replaced with the new season's plants. Thus early spring bulbs can make way for a bright display of primula and polyanthus or colour co-ordinated pansies until it is time to plant out a selection of tender vegetables: tiny cherry tomatoes, miniature albino aubergines or startling yellow courgettes (*see Edibles, pages 64–65*).

Summer could see the introduction of large hanging baskets of strawberries or the outrageous *Begonia pendula*; or one of the more extravagant pendulous fuchsia hybrids. Follow this into autumn with a display of autumn-flowering bulbs or a collection of pot chrysanthemums. The beauty of this ever-changing, portable display is that it can always be kept looking in peak condition, to give the conservatory that special lift whenever it needs it; plants can also be changed from year to year, offering the chance to try out new combinations and new varieties.

Bulbs are ideal candidates for this kind of *ad hoc* treatment of course, for while their fresh colours and scents are more than welcome at times of the year when little else is coming into its own, you won't want them taking up precious space in your beds and containers during their lengthy dormant and dying back stages. Once flowers have been forced, you cannot use them to flower indoors the following year, so they should be ripened off and planted in the garden.

Fig 63 Zantedeschia aethiopica.

However, tender bulbs such as *Freesia*, *Nerine* and *Vallota* can be cultivated in the conservatory and allowed to bloom *in situ* for several years.

For your containers, extend your planting plans beyond the early spring narcissi, crocus, chionodoxa and sweet scented hyacinths, a lovely and welcome sight as they are, to include more exotic flowering bulbs to enhance your basic planting scheme: lilies can look wonderful in crusty old terracotta pots or glazed ceramic planters, too valuable for the garden or patio but perfectly at home standing on the conservatory floor amongst your best dramatic foliage specimens and cane furniture. Queen of the lilies, and deserving your finest container is the Madonna Lily, *Lilium auratum*, which produces pure white clusters of blooms with gold centres; or if your conservatory has a definite jungle atmosphere and your pots will be standing among giant palm-like plants, yucca and banana plants (*Musa*), select the tawny Tiger Lily, *Lilium tigrinum*, with its distinctive gold speckled blooms. Either of these can be forced to bloom at any time of the year – a great lift to the spirits during the darker months of winter. The Scarborough Lily, *Vallota speciosa*, is designed to bloom in late summer, producing an excellent show of scarlet trumpets; the Arum Lily, *Zantedeschia aethiopica*, is more of a spring flowering spectacular, with huge white trumpet blooms against arrow-shaped foliage. Equally grand and very like a lily in the shape and style of its blooms is the stately *Hippeastrum* which bears its brightly coloured trumpets on a single stem as tall as 50–70cm/20–28in. If you find the pinks and scarlets a little too showy, choose one of the white-flowering hybrids like 'Nirvalis', a more delicate flower with a yellow centre.

More permanent planting of shrubs and perennial plants can provide regular highlights throughout the year in beds or large containers. Particularly good value are handsome evergreens like Camellia or *Cassia corymbosa*, which can offer the bonus of attractive foliage all year, as well as the most beautiful blooms: glossy green foliage in the case of Camellia, delicate and

Fig 64 Callistemon viminalis.

frondy for Cassia. These are the sort of plants you should be looking for if short of space or when seeking maximum visual impact from your plants for minimum maintenance. Summer or winter, the cool conservatory can maintain an excellent display with an exotic cockspur-coral tree, *Erythrina crista-galli*, whose glossy green leaves are set on fire in summer with waxy red blooms; feathery green Bottle Brush, *Callistemon*, with its unusual brush-like flowers, also a brilliant red; the bushy evergreen *Carpenteria californica*, a popular hibiscus, both making an unrivalled spectacle of flowers in summer; or enjoy the sight of a small tree like *Sparmannia africana* covering itself in white summer flowers.

Fill in the gaps with trusty pelargoniums, reliably hardy and offering a huge choice of in-

Fig 65 (Below) *Flowering plants bought at your local nursery or garden centre can be used to add seasonal colour.*

teresting foliage and flower forms including spicy scented leaf varieties that will subtly scent the conservatory with all the old-fashioned rose, clove, lemon and mint flavours of a pot-pourri. For highlights in winter among the evergreen foliage, there is an equally wide and varied choice: the bright yellow fluffy buttons of mimosa, *Acacia dealbata*, with its haunting fragrance; *Luculia gratissima*, a small tree making a mass of scented pink flowers; or one of the autumn/winter flowering heathers like *Erica gracilis*, which produces clusters of pink and white bells.

A little artificial heat might extend your scope to include even more exotic flowering species, such as Angel's Trumpet, *Datura cornigera*, with its unexpectedly scented hanging trumpets; the yellow spotted bells of *Smithiantha cinnabarina*; or the evergreen *Ixora coccinea*'s large red clusters. While for winter, there are late-flowering shrubs like Egyptian Star Cluster, *Pentas lanceolata*, producing unusual balls of star-shaped, pink flowers.

Scent is important in the conservatory; it is part of its charm to expect the fragrance of scented foliage and flowers, subtly altered as plants change through the seasons, to be heightened and mingled like a living pot-pourri by the build-up of heat under glass and the humidity achieved by keeping plants well sprayed and watered. Many of the flowering species we have already mentioned are scented and there are more – tender gardenia, another winter bloomer by the way, is a well-loved favourite, as is heady Cherry Pie, *Heliotropium arborescens*. It should be possible to select a succession of scents to keep the conservatory sweet throughout the year.

THE INDOOR WATER GARDEN

A water feature, whether it be a small pool, complete with fountain, a simple wall-mounted water spout pouring into a shallow bowl, a free-standing water sculpture or a bubble fountain

Fig 66   Water-lily.

where the water gurgles over stones or pebbles into a concealed reservoir, makes an attractive and practical addition to the conservatory. Moving water releases moisture into the air and helps create a more humid atmosphere in an area that tends to be at risk from being overheated and dry; you may find that you can grow cool moisture-lovers such as ferns or ivies beside a pool, and there are various exciting water plants worth adding to your conservatory collection. A pool makes an excellent focal point and can be raised or sunk into the floor, constructed using a tough butyl liner or purchased ready-made in moulded fibreglass. It is the perfect opportunity to display one or more tropical water-lilies which hold their flowers proud above the water and those familiar flat leafy pad plants such as *Nymphaea capensis*, the night flowering *N. lotus*, or *N. stellata*, and their derivatives, are all suitable, as is the large-bloomed *Nelumbo nocifera* in shades of pink or white.

Many of the dramatic poolside plants that grow outdoors will also do well beside the indoor pool, planted on a marginal shelf just below the surface of the water, or in nearby tubs, providing the compost can be kept moist. Bamboos, and the rush *Cyperus*, have tall stems topped with grassy foliage which look very stylish, especially in large, glazed Chinese ginger jars which lend them an oriental air. Another attractive plant for the surface of the water itself is the normally rampant Water Hyacinth, *Eichhornia crassipes*, which has lovely flower spikes of mauve and gold. If you are planning a pool and are prepared to heat it with a small pool-heater unit, you could also include a few interesting tropical fish such as guppies or gouramis; but even an unheated pool indoors would be suitable for the less hardy goldfish like shubunkins, comets and moors.

Should you find your indoor pool becomes murky and suffers from algae problems (a common complaint), the quickest way to cure it is to install a small water filter. This can be run from the same power source as your heater or fountain, and it guarantees sparkling clear water, resulting in hours of pleasure lazily observing fish or plants. Any electrical installation in or near water should be of the low-voltage type for safety, including plant spotlights and underwater lighting.

EDIBLE PLANTS

Conservatory conditions are ideal for certain fruits and vegetables that are just a little too tender to ripen properly outdoors; if you choose the more ornamental types and varieties and plant them in attractive troughs, pots and containers, you will combine a fine collection of plants with the pleasure of sampling your own produce, ripened right under your nose. With special pocketed planters or hanging baskets sprouting with scarlet strawberries and tiny cherry tomatoes, tubs and troughs of green plants weighed down by glossy peppers, auber-

Fig 67 Citrus clementina.

gines and courgettes, there is no danger of a mundane greenhouse atmosphere invading your sophisticated conservatory.

Keep plants strictly under control and select the smaller, more decorative varieties, like the aubergine *Solanum melongena* 'Bonica', which is compact and bushy, or 'Easter Egg', a miniature white aubergine guaranteed to be a talking point both in the conservatory and at the dining table. Courgettes do well in the warmth of a conservatory, but they should be picked when they are about the size of your index finger; there is a yellow form, Gold Rush, which is particularly attractive. Others which positively benefit from the light and warmth are sweet peppers, ripening to red, green, purple, yellow or white according to type and as decorative as any ornamental fruiting plant, and tomatoes. The compact, small fruiting hybrids are neatest and often sweetest, growing well in pots, or even hanging baskets providing you can keep the plants well watered.

Some fruits are also naturally good choices for conservatory cultivation. Figs, grapes, peaches, nectarines, apricots and melons are all good examples, plants our ancestors grew in their hothouses. The grander or more enthusiastic estates had individual glasshouses, not just for separate fruits, but even for individual fruit types – an early peach house, a mid-season apricot house, and so on. We are more likely to experiment with a couple of varieties for fun: a single grapevine in a cool conservatory, a vigorous fig or, perfectly at home in a hot, dry atmosphere, sweet melons. In a limited space, soft fruits such as peaches, apricots and nectarines can be grown very successfully layered against a wall or constrained within tubs, trained into compact standard tree or espalier shapes.

Most successful and, again, a familiar element of the traditional conservatory, are small citrus trees: oranges or lemons look very pretty in an ornamental tub or pot with their neat evergreen foliage, sweet-scented flowers and brilliant fruits. Trees are frequently placed outside on a warm patio or terrace during the summer months and will do well given plenty of light and cool winter temperatures.

Fig 68   A grapevine climbing up a trellis.

SPECIAL COLLECTIONS

Plants with quite specific needs, which have evolved to meet the stringent requirements of their natural environment, whether that be a dry and dusty desert exposed to harsh, unrelenting sunshine or the moist, shady conditions of a forest floor, can be difficult to incorporate into a mixed plant group. Their needs are so exacting that they simply cannot survive too great a variation in temperature, light or humidity. However keenly you wish to grow a particular specimen for its fine shape, colour and habit, this type of plant just is not going to oblige you unless you satisfy its every need.

There are borderline cases, but generally speaking, if you are mad about orchids, cacti or ferns, your best approach is to start a specific plant collection within your favoured group. That way you can provide, as closely as possible, the correct environment and requirements for the whole group. While a conservatory provides the opportunity to control most of these parameters artificially, it helps if you are not fighting completely against the odds by trying to grow shade-lovers in a south-facing, scorching sun trap, or vice versa.

Special collections usually involve the real shade and moisture lovers like ferns and ivies which offer such a wonderful range of foliage options, but which just are not practical to keep in the average conservatory. However, if you happen to have an unheated, north-facing conservatory, they will do very well indeed and you would be advised to make full use of their natural attributes and the design possibilities they can offer for large and small specimens, dwarf forms, unusual shapes and climbers.

Ferns

Ferns are undeniably graceful, frondy foliage plants, some of which are feathery and delicate, others more robust. There are even some species which have lusher, glossy leaves. Ferns must have shade and they must have humidity;

65

Fig 69 Adiantum cuneatum.

grouping them together can help conserve moisture levels, as will plunging the pots in damp peat or moss. A gravel tray or trough beneath a collection of pots can be kept wet to aid watering, for while the compost should never be allowed to dry out, the roots will rot if they become water logged.

Individual species can look very dramatic and stylish confined to a hanging basket or pot, or allowed to trail over a shelf or free-standing pillar. The ferns' subtle shades of green with maybe a touch of bronze and the variation of shapes look very attractive when a selection of different types are arranged on staging at different levels. You will soon know if your ferns are receiving too much light as they will start to lose their colour and vigour.

You can create some interesting contrasts between ferns like the tiny moss-like creeper *Selaginalla*, the arching green fronds of a Maiden

Hair Fern, *Adiantum*, or the exotic Staghorn Fern, *Platycerium*, which looks like a pair of green antlers. There are many similar forms: the Boston Fern, *Nephrolepis exalta* 'Bostoniensis', is particularly suited to hanging baskets with its cascading arrangement of bright green fronds. The Bird's-nest Fern, *Asplenium nidus*, is different from the rest, with undivided glossy leaves that can be used for contrasts alongside specimens with more divided, delicate fronds. There are a couple of ferns which will tolerate drier, warmer conditions should you wish to include them in a mixed arrangement. *Cyrtomium falcatum* has rather loosely arranged glossy evergreen fronds; *Pellaea rotundifolia* displays unusual small circular leaves on string-like stems.

Good companions for hardy ferns in that they share similar climate likes and dislikes are the ivies, and happily their climbing, small-leaved, usually glossy foliage is an excellent foil for the fern's extravagant featheriness. There are a great many decorative hybrids for training up supports or allowing to cascade over shelves or out of pots. Leaves may be large or small, heart- or arrow-shaped, green or gold. There is also an excellent variety of variegated forms with bands, spots, splashes and borders in white, cream, silver or gold.

Palms

Palms, another plant which cannot survive without high levels of moisture and a humid atmosphere, flourish in damp conditions and do not mind shade although they do like a reasonable amount of light and cool temperatures – around 7°C/45°F in winter. They always look so fine and elegant with their large palmate leaves or more delicate feathery fronds, that they are guaranteed to add an air of gentility to an interior or a touch of drama to a planting scheme. Palms are happiest in small containers, and providing they are well watered and the leaves are sprayed regularly, they do not require a lot of attention.

The range of shapes and styles within the

Fig 70   Phoenix robellinii.

group is quite surprising when you get to know them better, from the pretty dwarf palm *Cocos* to the classic Kentia Palm, *Howeia*, which cannot tolerate hot, dry conditions at all, or the fan-shaped display of leathery leaves of *Raphis excelsa*. The length of the stems and the spread of the rough and prickly or finely cut foliage determines the different effects – these are plants which look particularly good when lit by spot-lamps from below to create interesting shadows and contrasts.

Cacti

Going to the opposite extreme, if you have a hot, dry, sunny south-facing conservatory, you will have the perfect environment for a collection of cacti. These are plants for lovers of the bizarre, since most of them do not look like plants at all but resemble pebbles, pin cushions or bundles of fluff, and it is only when the brilliant, unreal

flowers appear that they give any sign of being a living object. Their swollen stems are designed to hold water in drought conditions and all those spines, bristles, hairs and tufts (called areoles), are part of the cacti's protective mechanism. They will take a remarkable amount of neglect, but will not survive damp or cold. A deep container is better than a shallow one and you should make sure that drainage is as efficient as possible by filling the bottom with broken crocks and about 9cm/4in of washed gravel. Cacti make good conservatory plants, needing very little care apart from good light and good ventilation. Do not worry about temperature during the summer months, but cacti do like cooler temperatures in the winter, no more than 6°C/43°F. To encourage flowering they should not be watered at all during the winter period.

Although all the forms seem rather strange, cacti do fall into a series of quite distinct groups according to their general shape and appearance – and a selection of several of these will make a fine collection. Some grow quite tall, as big as trees in the wild, while others are almost miniature forms and can be used to create mini cacti gardens in a trough or bowl. Best known is perhaps the Prickly Pear, *Opuntia*, which includes many species of cylindrical and flat jointed segments with all kinds of colourful features such as red aerioles, white spines or yellow flowers. Equally popular is the Hedgehog Cactus, *Echinocactus*, which is particularly round and prickly and produces a wide variety of interesting flowers. Watering before the weather gets warmer will encourage the flowers to form; some species in the group are very free-flowering producing exotic and brightly coloured blooms including night-flowering types called *Notocactus*.

More easily recognised and easy to grow, although slow and susceptible to fungal rot, is the large *Mammillaria* group of cacti which have prominant tubercles and an interesting range of flowers. There are a great many individual species in this particular genus including some interesting colour variations such as the white-

Fig 71 Many different species of cacti will thrive in the conservatory.

flowers along long thin stems. Another in-teresting group is *Astrophytum*, which includes both spiny and spineless forms, with names like Bishop's Mitre and Bishop's Cap to describe their strange, round appearance and different coloured features such as spines, flowers and scales. Surprisingly perhaps, some of the flowers are scented, for example 'Cereus', which is easy to grow and blooms at night.

If you intend to grow a mixed group of semi-desert and forest cacti, you will have to separate them since the epiphytes, or forest type, do not require full sunlight, unlike the others. They can be placed on the shelving below if using staging, or in floor-standing containers, for these are cacti which require some shade. Although tolerant of neglect, you can't ignore them completely – cacti do require some attention to flourish. Getting the watering right can be tricky; desert cacti should not be watered at all during the winter, but in the summer they should be given plenty – when the soil has become completely dry. It is important to make sure that the plant is never actually standing in water. The best time to water is in the early morning before the sun gets too hot; never water 'little and often' but give a pro-per soaking when the soil is dry.

spined *M. plumosa*, the yellow spines and red flowers of *M. spinosissima*, and dark green *M. zeilmanniana*, which has reddish-purple flowers. Forest Cacti are completely different again, they have a more flattened form which looks almost like real leaves, and they produce large showy flowers from the tips. Best known is probably the Christmas Cactus, *Zygocactus truncatus*, which like others in this group do not need the com-mon winter resting period and can almost be treated like a normal house plant.

There are even some climbing forms of cacti which are self-supporting by means of aerial roots, although the stems bend easily and the plants are best staked or grown up the conser-vatory wall. All produce beautiful flowers, usually at night. Most popular is the Rat's Tail Cactus, *Aporocactus flagelliformis*, which produces pink

Orchids

One of the most exciting opportunities a conser-vatory can offer is the chance to build up a collec-tion of orchids, plants so beautiful and delicate that many find it hard to believe just how easy they are to grow. This is due to modern breeding and the introduction of some thirty thousand hybrids, each of which seems more lovely than the last, and which no longer require humid jungle conditions to grow successfully. Orchids comprise one of the largest families in the plant kingdom, but while most of the twenty-five thou-sand wild species are terrestrial, that is, rooted in the ground, most cultivated orchids have been developed from epiphytic or air plant types.

Fig 72 (Opposite)   Cymbidium orchid.

These gain nourishment and moisture from the air and are usually rooted on trees or bushes in tropical or sub-tropical regions. It is the epiphytes which have the loveliest flowers and today's hybrids have been specially developed from them to suit the more artificial conditions of the greenhouse or conservatory.

Orchids need plenty of light, but not direct sunlight and fall roughly into three temperature bands, as indicated on page 119. Most like to rest during the winter months but during the summer season when the plant is growing it should be fed and the compost freely watered to keep it permanently moist. Good ventilation is equally essential, and humidity levels should be kept high during the summer by spraying the plants or by hosing down the floor of the conservatory. During the resting stage, orchids need to be positioned in full light and kept dry until new growth appears. Bark chippings are usually used as compost, being closest to the orchid's natural environment, and plants should be repotted every alternate year. Orchids prefer small pots to large ones, and some have to be grown in special slatted containers because they bloom from the bottom of the compost.

There are a great many different shapes, colours and types, many of which look like some kind of strange insect, with distinct striped and spotted petals and a large, attractive lip. This often forms a striking contrast to colour and pattern, but is really designed as a landing platform for pollen collectors. They are fascinating plants, not just because of their strangely modified appearance, nor simply because their reproductive process is unique; there are just so many interesting types, from real miniatures to large specimens producing only one bloom. In fact, it can be difficult to know where to start when making a collection. The range might run from a winter-flowering species like the green-and-white flowered *Angraecum eburneum*, which is unusual in that it should be watered throughout the year, to the spring- and summer-flowering *Phalaenopsis lueddemanniana*, which will produce several flower spikes smothered in white or yellow flowers, marked with pink or purple. There are many orchids that flower in autumn and winter, enabling you to plan a spectacular all-year-round display; quite a few are irresistably scented, others smell foul but will bewitch you with their extraordinary range of colours or delicate form.

You should select plants from one temperature group only, so that they will all be compatible, and you will know exactly what conditions you have to provide. Standing your plants just above a tray of wet gravel over your heat source will help increase humidity. Orchids like fresh air but they hate draughts, so a small fan may be necessary to keep the air moving; most require plenty of light but not direct sunlight – artificial lighting may have to be employed via fluorescent tubes to act as a booster since plants will require at least ten hours of light daily, but no more than sixteen hours as this will prevent your orchids from flowering. It will help if you turn the pots occasionally so that they grow evenly. The correct daytime temperature is important, but orchids are fussy about the night as well – a drop of around 5°C/10°F is quite important and plants may have to be moved to a cooler part of the house if this is not possible in the conservatory. Large, heavy flower heads may need supporting by tying to stakes – but not the base-flowering types like the pendulous *Cymbidium*, which should be allowed to hang down from a suspended basket.

Care and Maintenance

The well-stocked conservatory with a carefully planned display of flowering and foliage plants relies on routine care and a healthy environment to remain looking good. While the sight of flourishing, happy plants *en masse* is exciting and a pleasure to contemplate, the appearance of just a couple of sickly specimens, or the non-removal of dead and diseased material quickly spoils the effect. Unchecked, the situation will only worsen in such an enclosed, close community, pests and diseases spreading with frightening speed from plant to plant and transforming your thriving jungle into a sorry scene of desolation. Unfortunately, the extremely hot, dry conditions of most conservatories will quickly take their toll of neglected plants and encourage the development of bugs such as red spider mite; once leaves and stems begin to wilt and die, disease sets in.

It certainly pays to get off to a good start with the finest, healthiest specimens you can beg, buy or propagate. To keep them healthy you should make sure you know the practical requirements of every one, so that you can position them where they will be happiest. Only by familiarising yourself with the approximate light, heat and humidity needs of your collection can you keep them contented. This need not be time-consuming or a burden — with automatic shading, ventilation and even watering systems available their care can become part of your daily routine, in fact no more bother than ensuring your house plants are adequately watered. While carrying out general plant maintenance, it is also a good idea to keep an eye open for any signs of disease or pest infestation so that it can

be dealt with properly and thus prevent the problem getting out of control. The guidelines in this chapter should keep your conservatory collection in prime condition.

CHOOSING AND BUYING YOUR PLANTS

Unless you want to start your conservatory off as a room more akin to a plant hospital, or you are prepared to spend the time and trouble nursing below par plants to good health, you should ensure that you start your plant collection with the very best specimens you can get your hands on. This not only gets the conservatory off to a good

Fig 73   The beauty of conservatory gardening is that you get maximum effect for very little effort. You will not need a lot of expensive tools or accessories; a small trowel and fork, a dibber for planting bulbs, secateurs, and for tall plants, some form of support.

start, it avoids making problems for the future. You are creating a very special environment, one that is highly concentrated, with plants in close proximity to each other which could so easily develop into a potential hotbed of problems.

Firstly you should make sure you are ready for your plants. It is easy to get carried away by enthusiasm for all these lovely exotic species you will have been reading about and maybe seeing in photographs, or enjoying at local plant centres and the grand glass houses open to the public. However, do try to be patient, for the majority of plants dislike the disruption of any sudden change to their growing environment. It helps to have their new home ready and waiting so that they can adjust properly to their new surroundings without further distress. The worst thing you could do is buy a huge load of plants and leave them stacked together in a draughty hallway, shed or garage, while your conservatory interior is being completed.

The time to start thinking about buying your plants is when the builders have gone and planting beds and containers are ready, full of compost. Plants are expensive, especially large ones or rare, imported exotics so you may be looking for ways to cut down on cost. Beware of cheap plant bargains – they are often a false economy and if you are tempted to purchase specimens from street markets, outside vegetable shops or road-side vendors, be prepared for the worst. It is more reassuring and makes better sense to get your plants from someone you know has cared for them and, indeed, understands them, such as a specialist nursery or plant centre.

Sometimes large indoor plants can be obtained inexpensively from modern offices on the move, or from companies who are reorganising their office space. There may be some good bargains to be had among the bolder architectural foliage plants, but you will have to use your discretion on whether their condition merits the reduced cost, since plants in commercial situations seem either extremely well cared for or dreadfully neglected: presumably this is dependant on the enthusiasm of the employees.

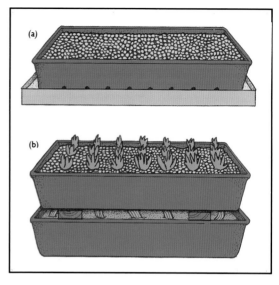

Fig 74 Home hydroponics. (a) Propagate your own flowering plants from existing stock to boost your conservatory display, or to provide material for exchange, using hydroponic methods. Cuttings are rooted in a tray of sterile soil substitute (such as vermiculite or perlite). A balanced nutrient solution is added each day and allowed to drain through holes in the sloped tray to the dish below. Drained solution can be re-used. (b) Even more convenient is a wick-fed system where the nutrient solution is fed into the plant tray by capillary action through synthetic wicks over a period of about two weeks.

Since a large collection can be costly, one way to reduce that cost is to beg, buy or exchange plants with like-minded friends. Once your collection gets going and plants are thriving, you may like to experiment with propagating, producing healthy new plants from cuttings to provide yourself with material for barter. Some plants for the conservatory can be grown from seed if you have the patience. Never take cuttings from homes and gardens that you visit without asking permission. This is not only very bad manners, but cuttings hastily made and concealed rarely thrive. Often you will find that if you profess a genuine interest, owners are only too happy to let you have a piece (it is always worth keeping a

Fig 75   Plants arranged on professional staging can take full advantage of automatic watering and feeding systems.

stock of plastic bags and ties in your pocket in the event of a generous offer).

A tour of your local plant centres will give you some idea of which have the best selection and keep their plants in first class condition. The firm may be well established or even a specialist in the type of plant you are looking for, but you can usually see at a glance if plants are healthy and growing well and if stocks are being well maintained. If you are hoping to start a collection of a certain type of plant, such as orchids, ferns or palms, you would be advised to seek out a specialist nursery who will be familiar with their special requirements, have a better selection and be able to offer valid advice. Another point to watch for is whether plants are well labelled and attractively displayed. It is to your advantage to gain as

much information as possible about the plant from your supplier – suitable compost for repotting, food and watering needs and any special problems to look out for. Some of the better garden centres are making the most of modern technology with computer-produced fact sheets for every plant purchased.

By all means wander round a well-stocked plant centre to give you some idea of the range of plants available and what they look like. But try to come back and buy on another day, list in hand. Plants bought on impulse are frequently a mistake and it is better to work out exactly what you need for your collection, or the space you are looking to fill, and buy accordingly. If you know exactly where the plant is going to go, you can not only install it there as soon as you get

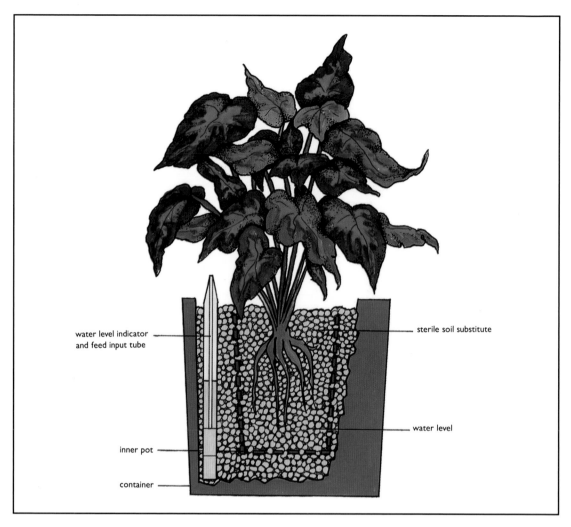

water level indicator and feed input tube

sterile soil substitute

water level

inner pot

container

Fig 76 You can buy a special pot for hydroculture which leaves you little
to do bar keep the water level topped up for around six months. The
hydroponic pot comprises a mesh inner container of sterile granules to
support the root system and an outer unit. The water level maintains the
nutrient solution 5cm/2in from the base

home, it will also ensure that you don't end up buying something totally unsuitable.

A little homework is well worth the time spent and a list in hand is a comfort when faced by a confusing array of greenery and busy assistants. It might be a good idea to start off your collection with the tougher, more tolerant species of plant which can be less susceptible to the effects of change and difficult conditions. This will not only give you confidence and help get your conservatory off to a good start, it will quickly establish

your mini conservatory climate, all the better for introducing more difficult, tender subjects into your scheme at the next stage.

When you have chosen your supplier and are ready to buy, make sure you have set plenty of time aside for the shopping trip. You will need to examine each particular plant very carefully to check it is in good condition. You will naturally be drawn to those plants which look healthiest — those with good glossy colour, bushy with plenty of new growth and no sign of pest or disease. You will already have researched the speed of growth and likely mature size of a particular species; size and ease of cultivation will naturally be reflected in the cost, and a small specimen of a slow or difficult grower may seem disproportionately expensive. Sad to say, it pays to shop around when buying from the majority of local garden centres; prices and standards can fluctuate wildly for identical plants. The maturity of your chosen plants will also affect your budget. Large specimens are very useful for creating an immediate effect if you can afford them, but younger plants will establish themselves more quickly, will adapt themselves more readily and, unless you are considering a particularly slow-growing species such as some of the palms, you will soon catch up. So the cost of a showy plant may not be worth it, particularly considering the extra transport problems you are giving yourself.

Avoid selecting plants for interiors that have obviously been standing outside or which are not displayed in an area that receives adequate light, heat and humidity. Examine individual specimens carefully and reject any that look straggly or sickly. Check the underside of leaves as well as the tops to make sure there are no pest infestations and look out for signs of yellowing, wilting or mottled and damaged foliage. Potted or container-grown plants are preferable since they transport more easily and seem to suffer less trauma when being installed in new surroundings. However, do check wherever possible that the plant has not been allowed to become potbound evident by some wilting of the leaves, too much plant and not enough compost in the pot, or by roots escaping from the bottom, sides or even top of the container. The soil should be moist and healthy-looking, never shrunk away from the side of the pot nor infested with moss. If buying trees, shrubs, vines or other climbers, check that they have been pruned or trained correctly and make sure you know what stage of development they are at. When buying flowering plants for instant seasonal display, it is best to choose them in the early stages of budding and bring them into flower at home. This will not only

protect blooms in transit, but gives you the best of their display.

With your plants chosen and paid for, you should aim to get them home with minimum trauma. If you can, buy your plants during warm weather when they are less likely to be damaged by the sudden change in temperature between garden centre or nursery greenhouse, and your conservatory. If the weather outside has dropped below freezing, you are advised to buy after it has warmed up a little rather than risk your plants catching cold. Try to organise things so that the plant spends the least possible amount of time travelling. You should take it straight home; do not go shopping or out for the afternoon, leaving plants to suffer in the back of your car or trailer. Correct packing can also help to minimise damage to foliage, stems and roots. Small plants in pots can be laid carefully on their side in card-

Fig 77 Check out your local garden centre for top-quality, healthy looking plants.

board boxes surrounded by damp compost, with damp newspaper wedged in between them to keep them in place. Plants with large foliage can have their leaves tied loosely to a supporting stick or stake to reduce their size and protect them from damage. Ideally, plants should not be in full flower, as flower (and leaf) buds are easily damaged.

Sometimes plants are not supplied in pots and care should be taken not to damage the root ball by keeping as much earth around it as possible. Ensure this is well dampened and enclose it in a plastic bag. Large plants can be seriously affected by damage to the roots, so again make sure there is plenty of earth around the root ball and firmly tie a piece of sacking around it. A large plastic bag over the whole plant will help prevent it from being damaged by wind, cold or accidental knocks in transit; particularly delicate specimens can be protected by a plastic bag held away from the foliage by canes or sticks.

As soon as you get home, carry plants carefully into the house and straight into the conservatory. Unwrap carefully and check for damage, pruning where necessary and watering or spraying with warm water if the compost has dried out or if the plant is looking wilted. Its new position should be already prepared and the temperature in your conservatory should be as close as possible to the environment it has just left. Re-plant carefully in its new bed or container at the earliest opportunity and keep a close eye on its progress for a week or two to make sure you are giving it the right conditions and that no infestations develop.

PLANT CARE

Your newly established, hopefully happy, plants will only thrive if they are given, as closely as possible, the light, temperature and moisture conditions that they are used to in their natural environment. They will also need to be fed occasionally with the right kind of compost and fertiliser. Plants, containers and the surrounding area must also be kept clean to prevent a build-up of disease.

LET THERE BE LIGHT

All plants need light to function properly and to photosynthesise; but their natural requirements will vary widely from cacti, which will soak up all the sunshine they can get, to plants like fittonias which grow on the floor of the tropical rain-forests and normally receive only about five per cent of available daily light. A plant used to shady conditions will wilt, or the leaves drop if there is too much light; too little light for a sun-lover produces a spindly, weak plant with a sickly pale appearance. You will have checked the light requirements of your individual specimens and will be aware that light levels in a conservatory tend to be exceptionally high. Very few plants can tolerate these conditions and some form of shading will be necessary (see pages 33–35).

We have already discussed how the position of your conservatory and its orientation will determine to some extent the strength of the light it will receive, and you will have grasped some idea of the range of plants that will flourish there. You may also have planned areas for shadier environment species by filtering the light with large shrubs or climbers, or by installing staggered staging to enable these plants to be positioned on the lower shelves. Containers can also be positioned where they will receive less light. Even in a conservatory the amount of light from the sun decreases as you move away from the windows, especially if the roof is screened – which it will be for a large amount of the time for both you and your plant's comfort. The light diminishes by 1–2 per cent for every metre/3 ft away from the source of light. Screens and blinds may reduce light intensity (but not necessarily heat) by around 50 per cent; this produces a reduction of 20–25 per cent further from the light source. These levels are significantly reduced within a north-facing conservatory; east- or west-facing structures receive periods of strong sunshine only

Fig 78 *Plants grown in bright light nearest the window may grow unevenly. (a) Turning the pot round a third of a turn every couple of days will even out growth. (b) Left lit from the one side only, plants will develop a nasty lean and distorted foliage. (c) Some flowering plants like chrysanthemums do not like too much sun and should be allowed no more than twelve hours of light per day. (d) Too much light will make new growth spindly and blooms sparse.*

at certain times of the day (first thing in the morning or towards the end of the afternoon). Remember, too, that the sun will be at least twice as bright in the summer as in winter. If you wish to check available light for any specific area and judge its suitability for a particular plant (say, of a plant by the conservatory windows or a container well to the rear of the room), use a light meter. There are several models specially developed for plant owners, which work on the same principal as a photographer's light meter.

Conservatories generally provide a fairly good all-round light. However, plants positioned close to the window may grow unevenly and bend stem and leaves towards the source of light, away from the room, which is exactly what you don't want them to do if you want to sit and enjoy them from inside. Many plants will naturally reorientate their foliage towards the light source to ensure that each leaf receives sufficient light. Where this does not happen, leaves will be facing the wrong direction and you may have to turn the plants on a regular basis to maintain even growth and display.

There are some plants that will require more light than the sun can provide naturally, particularly in winter when light levels are reduced and the days are shorter. Tropical and sub-tropical species (such as some orchids) which are used to hours of light a day may need boosting with an artificial light source if they are to flourish and flower. There are various ways in which you can provide artificial light; in all cases, you should be careful not to provide too much light or this can exhaust and damage your plant. Artificial light can also be used to encourage plants to grow

Fig 79 Medinilla magnifica.

continuously without a rest period and many tropical foliage plants will respond to this treatment providing you continue to feed them adequately. However, other types such as cacti must have their rest phase during which light, heat, water and food can be considerably reduced.

Artificial lighting can take the form of special light bulbs or fluorescent tubes which may be used to supplement natural light, particularly in winter, by turning on for around four to six hours every evening for foliage plants, six to eight hours for flowering types or as required according to your plants' needs. As well as straight tubes in various lengths, flat panels and rings have been introduced for installing over plant groups in bowls or tubs. There are also tubes specially recommended for plant use and which give out most of their light in red and blue wavelengths, which the plants prefer. An electric timer switch can be incorporated so that plants receive their top-up dose automatically.

Ordinary household incandescent lights are less useful since they give out more heat than light and need to be positioned so close to the plants that they are in danger of scorching the foliage. A standard 150W bulb would have to be at least 75cm/30in from the plant to prevent this happening, or a 25W bulb, 30cm/12in away.

Special plant tubes and domestic fluorescent lights provide around 10W per foot length and for most sized plants two tubes 15cm/6in apart is generally required as minimum. To replace natural light they should be positioned around 30–60cm/12–24in above foliage plants, and 25–30cm/9–12in above flowering ones. You may have to experiment to get the right position for your tubes or bulbs, moving them 7.5cm/3in at a time. For large areas you will find one long tube better than two short ones since the middle section gives out more light. Place them too near and your plants will be scorched and stunted; too far away will lead to spindly stems, small sparse leaves and no flowers.

There are available in some countries special intensified fluorescent tubes, called very-high-output (VHO) tubes, particularly recommended for use with plants such as cacti and pelargoniums which enjoy plenty of hot sunshine. Some plants such as tuberous begonias require as much as twelve to sixteen hours of light a day to produce flower buds. A VHO tube will give out as much as 30W per 30cm (12in) length and costs proportionately about three times more to run than standard tubes. Tubes tend to lose effectiveness after their allotted life span, barely discernible but making some difference to your plants. They should be changed after about a year.

A little back-up lighting may be necessary for specialist plants, but you will want to keep it as unobtrusive as possible. Fluorescent tubes can be built neatly under shelves or staging to illuminate plants below, or fitted to any flat surface. Plant growth bulbs can be incorporated in special shades or spotlights suspended above relevant plants. Special illuminated plant stands are available with integral lighting should you be looking for a freestanding floor display.

Decorative lighting also plays an important part in the conservatory, especially if you will be using it extensively at night. Domestic lamps and

Fig 80   Artificial light.   (a) A free-standing plant support with integral lighting is useful for plant displays in dark corners or towards the rear of a semi-glazed conservatory.   (b) A fluorescent tube can be concealed behind a baffle on an upper shelf to provide plants with extra light as required.

spotlights, uplighters and downlighters are ideal for this situation and can be positioned to illuminate individual plants to create a focal point and interesting shadows, particularly around plants with strong foliage, such as palms. Some of the best effects are achieved by concealing a spotlight within a plant arrangement and these can come ready supplied with soil spike if required. Alternatively, plants can be lit from above by means of spotlights attached to the main structure of the conservatory. The new low-voltage halogen spotlights are particularly good for this since they produce a very directional beam of white light that gives the plants a good accurate colour.

Any electrical installation in a conservatory should be tackled by a skilled electrician and for safety, with all that water around, all connections must be properly waterproof and the system fitted with a trip switch or circuit breaker. It may be advisable to use outdoor-quality up- and downlighters in the conservatory, particularly since these come in such an excellent range of types and sizes these days.

THE HEAT IS ON

Maintaining exactly the right temperature in a conservatory can be tricky, especially if you are hoping to use the area for living in as well as for plants. For your own comfort, a reasonably constant temperature of between 15–12°C/60–70°F is acceptable and should be maintained in

79

autumn, winter and spring. These temperatures will happily suit a great many plants too, although you should remember that tender varieties will also need warmth during the night too, after you have retired to bed. For your plants' sake temperatures should not drop below 7°C/45°F in winter or at night generally. Maintaining such temperatures should not present too many problems using one of the heating systems suggested on pages 30–32, if they are used in conjunction with electronic timers. However, it can be much more difficult to prevent the temperature rising too high in summer with the conservatory catching and amplifying all available heat; this is where shades and ventilation will have to be employed for the comfort of both plants and people.

Another problem with maintaining a suitable temperature is controlling the accompanying humidity levels. We like our environment relatively dry, but only a few plants share our preference. Tropical and sub-tropical plants, for example, tend to become stunted and the foliage go brown at the edges. However, there are ways of providing your plants with humidity whilst keeping the main part of the room comfortable for human inhabitants, as we will see later (pages 86–88).

If you feel you can not afford to heat your conservatory, you will find it still serves as a warm haven for sitting and relaxing as soon as the sun shines, even on winter days. The only disadvantage (from your point of view) is that the temperature drops equally dramatically at night. If you are happy with a late-spring to early-autumn living area with occasional use on sunny winter days, there is still a wide choice of plants available to create that lush, leafy environment. These are plants that enjoy the heat in summer but do not need it in winter, such as hardy annuals, bulbs and heathers, dramatic hardy foliage plants such as some of the tougher palms or some of the more attractive flowering or foliage shrubs like Camellia or Fatsia japonica.

A cool conservatory is the perfect place to take advantage of the many beautiful ferns and ivies available, although these will need to be kept cool and damp during the summer months as well as in winter, and a collection of these is best suited to a north-facing conservatory. These are a special case, though, and generally plants in a cool conservatory do not like moist conditions during the cooler months so care should be taken not to water plants too enthusiastically or create a steamy environment, as this will encourage plants to rot. Take advantage of a cool conservatory to grow fruits such as grapes and peaches which lap up the sun in summer but prefer simply the shelter of an unheated glasshouse in winter.

If you would like to introduce a wider variety of plants yet are not too bothered about using it yourself twelve months of the year, you can still help your heating budget by maintaining a minimum temperature of between 4–10°C/40–50°F. This won't be too comfortable for sitting in, but will make it possible for you to keep a fair number of exotic plants like Clianthus, Passion Flower, Clivia and Cissus happy and thriving.

Fig 81 Clivia miniata.

The minimum winter temperature requirements of many tropical and sub-tropical plants can vary between 4–10°C/40–50°F, so do check individual requirements and plan accordingly.

If you are enthusiastic about a particular plant group, such as tropical plants requiring temperatures of at least 18–21°C/65–70°F and high humidity (not very comfortable for humans but perfect for orchids and other rainforest plants), or at the other extreme cool, damp-loving ferns (equally unsuited to living areas), and you don't want to construct a plant-only conservatory, consider creating a small, special area for them with the correct conditions, perhaps in a corner of the main conservatory or in an annexe off it with glazed doors between. This solution is more economical on heating bills too.

WATER, WATER EVERYWHERE

We all know water is essential to plants' survival but deciding exactly how much, when and where is enough to make anyone nervous, as we all have experience of plants dying from lack of it or, more frequently from being given too much. Just to make matters worse, different plants have widely varying needs, particularly in the conservatory where you might be growing such curiosities as desert cacti or lush Passion Flower with its exotic blooms. In the conservatory environment there is the added worry of whether the air itself is too dry, and humidity levels will have to be calculated and adjusted. Of course, you can check in advance on a plant's particular requirements but these will vary according to growing conditions, time of year and temperature – extreme conditions and a collection of rain forest plants might demand a humidity level of as much as 80 per cent. In spring and summer, for example, when plants are making most vigorous growth, they will need plenty of water; high levels of sunshine or a sunny position will also increase need. Add to this the fact that some plants require rest periods and the picture starts getting very complicated. Other factors which affect the

Fig 82   Ferns offer a wide and exotic variety of feathery shapes in the cool, damp conservatory.

rate of watering include the type of pot and compost the plant has been given, since peat-based composts dry out more quickly than soil-based ones and unglazed pots allow more moisture to escape through evaporation than glazed or plastic containers, and therefore will need more water. A hanging basket is even more prone to moisture loss and can be difficult to water successfully.

With so many factors affecting requirements throughout the year, you can only resign yourself to playing it by ear. Your plants will let you know if you have got it wrong by drooping or shrivelling – but it is better not to wait until they reach this condition as plants may take a long time to recover, and repeated abuse will cause them to die. There are various time-honoured ways in which you can tell whether a plant is drying out and it is a good idea to check pots every day. Tapping the pot to see if it gives a ringing tone, which indicates a dry compost, or a dull one if it is wet, was all very well when all our pots were clay ones, but plastic pots are better tested with a pencil or finger pushed down into the compost to see if the soil is damp. There are special indicator sticks available that change colour

Fig 83 The heated conservatory offers the chance to grow more tender exotics like the amazing looking Passion Flower, Passiflora.

according to moisture content, but far more convenient and accurate is a moisture meter which tells you exactly the moisture level on an easy-to-read scale.

To test moisture in the soil of a bed or border, use the same techniques and apply water to penetrate to a depth of around 15cm/6in (which represents approximately 27 litres of water per square metre/4.75 gallons per square yard). Badly dried out compost will shrink away from the sides of the pot and except in special circumstances (some plants need occasional drought conditions), you should not allow things to go this far, as pots will then have to be well soaked to restore correct moisture levels. Of course, assessing watering needs on a daily basis must also be tailored to plants' individual requirements and there are some which should not be watered until the compost has completely dried

out. Very few plants need watering when the soil is still waterlogged.

The water you use to refresh your plants may be more important than you think. Most plants prefer fairly acidic conditions. Some, like rhododendrons, azaleas and heathers will tolerate nothing else, and the high lime content of tap water in hard water areas can quickly cause plants to start looking sickly, and even retard growth. You will probably know if you live in a hard water area, because you have already experienced problems with pipes or kettle furring up, and with scaly deposits. Those who are unsure can do a simple test using a pH indicator strip. A water filter or softener is the most practical solution, especially if it also filters out the chlorine and fluoride – both of which are harmful to your plants. Water temperature can also be a shock from which some plants may have prob-

82

Fig 84   There are many ways in which you can keep your plants watered while you are away or too busy to care for them.   (a) The automatic water diffuser comprises a porous receptacle which is inserted in the soil and which will release moisture over a period of about two to three weeks.   (b) A length of bandage or special wick will transfer water to your plants out of a bowl by capillary action.   (c) Plunging the plant pot into a large container packed with damp peat helps retain moisture. (d) Sealing the plant in an air-tight plastic bag allows it to enjoy its own humid atmosphere and will keep it moist for some time.

lems recovering. Water taken straight from the tap in winter may be sufficient to arrest the growth of more tender species. Ideally it should be around the same temperature as the room. Leave it to stand in buckets for a couple of hours in the conservatory, or, usually more convenient, mix hot water with cold to approximately the required temperature. The best time to water is in the evening or first thing in the morning. If you can, incorporate a tap and basin in a corner of the conservatory; an old stone or ceramic sink is ideal. You will find it useful not just for watering plants, but also for washing pots and a hundred and one tasks that you'd rather not do in the house. Alternatively, install a large galvanised tank outside with a tap inside the conservatory.

Fig 85 *A collection of different cactus species, including* Cereus *and* Opuntia.

Fig 86 *The best type of watering-can for conservatory plants has a long spout and a fine spray rose. A mist sprayer is also useful for improving humidity and moistening foliage. Always have a separate sprayer for pesticides.*

The correct watering technique can also aid success. How much should be regulated according to need: a plant in the middle of its active growing season will need plenty, so drench the compost until it begins to seep from the base of the pot (make sure you empty the saucer after watering to prevent root rot). Not all plants enjoy this treatment, and those with more modest needs should be given just enough to moisten the soil right through but without losing any into the saucer. For plants which are resting or those which, like cacti, need very little water, you can wait until the top two-thirds of the compost have dried out, then moisten sparingly. Make sure you know plants' individual requirements at every stage of their growth cycle and if in doubt, go easy on the water as too much tends to do more damage more quickly than too little.

There are various successful methods by which the water can actually be administered; again, some are more suited to certain types of plants. For general use, however, you need a small, lightweight watering-can with a capacity of around 2.5 litres/½ gallon and a long, thin spout capable of directing the water exactly where you need it. Most plants can be watered directly on to the compost at the top, or by pouring into the tray at the bottom and allowing it to be absorbed gradually – a good method for large pots where the water won't percolate far enough down to water the compost thoroughly.

Self-watering pots may be worth considering for large plant specimens; these incorporate their own water reservoir and level indicator, and need to be refilled every three or four weeks, so they are ideal for conservatory owners who go away a lot. Some plants require specialist watering techniques: plants such as saintpaulias, with their dense crown of soft hairy leaves, are prone to rot and should be watered only by the saucer method. Alternatively, stand the pots in a bowl of water until the top of the compost appears damp. This type of plant benefits from standing in a trough or tray lined with damp stones or gravel. Bromeliads are another special case, forming a central rosette into which the water should be poured. Never leave water in the saucer of any plant, as this encourages rot.

Special Remedies

Should you allow a plant to become so dry that the compost has shrunk away from the rim of the pot, you may find water runs straight through the dried out soil ball and out of the bottom. The best emergency remedy is to immerse pot and plant in a bucket of water so that the water covers the top of the soil, and leave it all to soak until the air bubbles stop rising.

Hanging baskets are always a problem as their soil dries out so quickly, and watering often results in an inconvenient stream of water down the back of the neck. Ideally they should be lifted down and treated to the bucket-soaking technique described above. Alternatively, use a special porous terracotta irrigator which you insert in the compost and fill as required, the water leaking out gradually.

Should water stay at the top of the pot and not be absorbed by the potting compost, the surface layer may have formed a crust and should be broken up with a skewer or sharp stick. If this does not work, the soil may have become compacted and you will find you have to repot the plant.

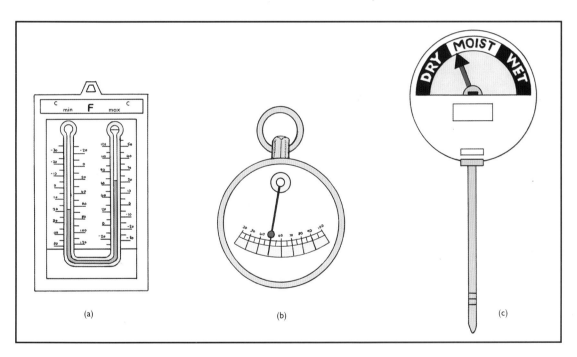

Fig 87 Temperature and moisture meters will take all the guess-work out of caring for plants with more specific needs. (a) A maximum/minimum thermometer is the best type, indicating highest and lowest temperature over a period of time. (b) A hygrometer indicates how much moisture there is in the air by showing the humidity percentage. You will definitely need one of these if you are growing tropical or sub-tropical species. (c) A simple moisture meter which you push down into the soil will save your plants from being over-watered and tell you for sure if the compost is too dry.

Fig 88 Aeonium sp.

Moisture in the Air

Correct air humidity in the conservatory is as essential as correct watering for your plants' survival, and the required levels are directly related to their particular needs and to the general temperature; the higher the temperature, the higher the level of humidity required. Tropical species, and ferns in cool conservatories, both need a very high humidity level, higher than is comfortable for human occupation and bringing with it further complications. The hotter the room the drier the air, and since conservatories encourage a hot, dry atmosphere naturally suited to very few plants save cacti, some remedial action will certainly be necessary. Again, it is essential to familiarise yourself with your plants' specific needs. Don't wait until you see the warning signs of excess dryness —

browning of leaf tips, drooping leaves, buds dropping off and flowers withering too quickly. Air humidity is measured on a scale from 0 to 100, 0 per cent being absolutely dry and 100 per cent being full saturation level. The average, undemanding plant requires a humidity level of at least 60 per cent, and more delicate species something close to 80 per cent. Even succulent plants require a level of 35–40 per cent and specialist plants in particularly hot, dry locations may require more.

Humidity can be measured on a hygrometer which shows the level on a simple dial and is well worth acquiring if you are serious about building up a conservatory collection. In the plant-only conservatory, humidity levels are increased by 'damping down', which involves splashing the floor with water and spraying foliage to prevent leaves losing water by transpiration. However, where the conservatory doubles as a living area this may not be practical, though we do recommend installing the kind of floor which can take this treatment occasionally, should it be required. The alternative is to spray foliage once or twice a day with a mist sprayer. Never spray in full sunshine or leaves may be scorched – the best time to spray is first thing in the morning.

There are other ways to increase humidity locally. Good ventilation will bring moist air into the conservatory from outside. Plants can also be encouraged to create their own microclimate by positioning them close together; water vapour transpired by the leaves will remain held by the interlocking foliage. However, like spraying the leaves, the effects are short-lived as the vapour eventually disappears into the dry atmosphere.

It helps to stand plants on a thin layer of pebbles, gravel or moisture-absorbing clay granules in a tray or saucer. The layer should be at least 2.5cm/ 1in deep and kept permanently moist, although the water should not be allowed to rise above the level of the pebbles and waterlog the roots. Alternatively, pack the pots into a deep-sided container padded with garden peat or sphagnum moss and keep this moist.

Another method for producing a humid microclimate around your plants is the use of capillary bolsters, which comprise a pad of water-absorbant granules which release the moisture gradually over a period of time. Placed in a container under the pot, they also cut down frequency of watering. All these methods work well where plants are sited over a source of heat.

If you have chosen plants which require a particularly high level of humidity, or your conservatory has a tendency to overheat and the air to become very dry, electric humidifiers are

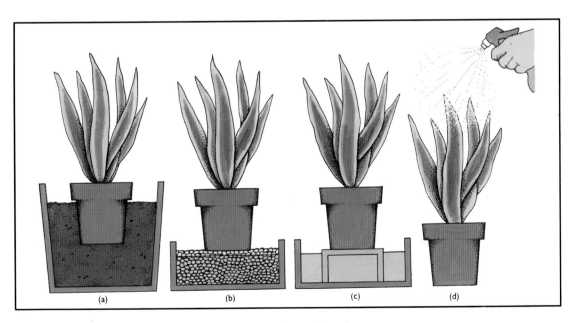

Fig 89   You can improve the humidity of individual plants by a variety of methods. Avoid increasing humidity levels during cold weather as it encourages disease.   (a) Bury the pot up to its rim in damp peat. (b) Stand pots on trays of wet gravel.   (c) Stand pots in bowls of water, making sure they are raised just above the water level.   (d) Mist spraying plants with softened water helps freshen foliage. However, do not spray plants in full sunlight, nor use hard water prone to lime scale as it will leave marks on the leaves.

available. Another automatic system worth considering, which automatically waters pots as well as improving air moisture, operates via a system of capillary benches instead of standard staging. Sand on the bench is kept damp using a water-feed device and the pots, directly on the sand, draw up moisture as required.

FOOD GLORIOUS FOOD

The right compost will have got your plant off to the right start, providing necessary minerals to be absorbed in the soil moisture by the roots. However, as the plant grows, those resources will become exhausted and in the enclosed conditions of a pot or container, even open beds, the plant will be unable to send out its roots to collect new food sources as it would in the wild. Therefore, conservatory plants will have to be fed artificially if they are to grow and flourish; you will find those in soil-based compost mixtures require feeding less often than those in peat-based.

A plant needs three main elements to grow and remain healthy: nitrogen, phosphorus and potassium. Nitrogen aids growth of foliage and new shoots, so is particularly necessary for leafy plants. Nitrogen is most needed at the start of the growing period, after a rest stage. Too much nitrogen immediately prior to resting, however, can be detrimental, producing too much growth before settling into a semi-dormant phase. Phosphorus aids the production of roots, so is important to young plants when they are struggling to establish themselves and to more mature specimens during flowering. Potash will keep plants healthy, improves resistance to disease, and is useful for improving yields of flowers and fruits. These elements in their pure form are not much good to your plants since they cannot be absorbed directly. Nitrogen is only useful in the form of nitrates, and equally, compounds such as phosphates and potash transform phosphorus and potassium into more accessible elements. In addition, smaller amounts of chemicals such as

Fig 90   Proper feeding results in a healthy conservatory collection.

iron and magnesium are required to aid the chlorophyll process.

Conservatory plants are best fed by means of specially prepared fertiliser compounds, and there are many variations available, often recommended for specific plant groups or to suit foliage or flowering types. Before you buy, it makes sense to check the individual requirements of specimens in your collection and calculate when and how often they will need the boost of a feed, as well as the type of fertiliser that will suit them best. As a rough guide, new or repotted plants should exist quite happily with what they have got for at least two months, unless potted in a loam-based potting mixture such as John Innes, in which case they will not need feeding for some time – at least until the root growth is well advanced.

Plants growing in peat-based composts will need feeding approximately once a fortnight

Fig 9l Aechmea tasciata.

during the growing season unless the plant has special needs. Some foliage plants, such as philodendron, only require a feed two or three times a year, unless you notice the leaves looking a little pale and yellow. Flowering climbers should also be fed carefully or they will produce a mass of foliage and no flowers. Other species are greedy feeders and need a regular supply of nutrients to keep pace with a rapid growth rate. The majority, though, require nutrients most immediately prior to leaf and flower production. Feeding every two weeks will encourage vigorous growth, and plants will require repotting once or maybe twice within a season. If you wish to reduce this rate of growth, cut the feed to every four to six weeks for plants in peat-based mixtures and every six or eight weeks for those in soil-based composts.

Do not feed from late winter to early spring when the plant should be resting; the results during a period of poor light and low temperatures will only be spindly and pallid. The only exception to this is those hot climate plants, whose growing season you can artificially extend by means of artificial lighting. Never feed sickly plants or those that have been allowed to become dehydrated in the hope that it will bring them round; wait until the specimen is looking stronger.

Fertiliser

There are two main types of fertiliser. The first, organic, includes garden compost, well-rotted manure, dried blood, bone meal and fish meal, all available in sterilised packs from garden centres. The second, chemical compounds, contain all the necessary nutrients in the correct proportions in liquid, powder and pellet form. Organic fertilisers which have to be activated by bacteria in the soil take longer to work, and easy-to-use synthetics which also come in smaller quantities, are usually preferred for indoor plants. The balanced chemical fertilisers act quickly, especially if using the liquid form which is directly absorbed through the plant's roots in solution. However, the slower acting organic fertilisers

provide a more complex mix of chemicals and are longer lasting.

The most popular organic fertiliser is dried blood, which provides a quick and generous dose of nitrogen. Hoof and horn is also good but is a slower source of nitrogen; bone meal and fish meal provide phosphate with a little nitrogen and potash; wood ash is a good source of potassium. Well-rotted manure or garden compost will supply a whole range of nutrients, and some gardeners like to supplement this with dried seaweed which is rich in trace elements and is available in powder or granular form. Chemical fertilisers offer the choice of buying and applying individual or combined nutrients, such as nitrates to provide nitrogen, and phosphorus-rich super-phosphates to supply potash. Most popular, though, are compound fertilisers which often blend both organic and synthetic elements to provide a balanced plant food. The elements are usually adjusted to suit the needs of different plant types, and appear as N for nitrogen, P for phosphorus and K for potash. The levels of each element in the fertiliser is indicated simply by three numbers, representing the percentage content, for example 8–6–10, which indicates 8 per cent nitrogen, 6 per cent phosphorus, and 10 per cent potash (the elements are always listed in this order). Plants in pots, whose roots are restricted, usually prefer a nitrogen-rich mixture, but potash is good for flowering plants. Adjust the levels according to plant needs and time of year.

Always follow manufacturers' instructions closely when applying fertiliser, particularly their recommendations for dilution. Feeding at lower than the recommended dose is preferable to a mix which is too strong, as this would damage your plants. It is important not to feed plants more than is necessary, since this not only tires them, but creates a build-up of damaging salts around the roots. There are various ways of applying fertiliser, according to type. Powder and granular fertilisers are designed to be scattered

Fig 92 (Opposite) Dieffenbachia 'Camilla'.

on the surface of the potting mixture and worked lightly in or added to the drip tray. This may not be the most convenient type for young, growing plants, but for older, well-established specimens in large pots a top dressing at the beginning of the growing season is often all they need. Alternatively you could remove the top few centimetres (about 1–2in) of compost and replace it with new plus the addition of your fertiliser.

Also useful for long-term, slow-release feeding are the capsules and pellets you can buy which are simply pushed into the soil and left to dissolve slowly. The fastest and easiest method of applying fertiliser are liquid feeds which are available as powder, crystals or concentrated liquid to be diluted in water. Nutrients are thus conveniently applied at the same time as watering. Generally, fertilisers are applied as close to the roots as possible and kept well away from the leaves, which would be damaged by contact with them.

Fig 93 Dracaena fragrans *'Massangeana'.*

However, in some cases a foliar feed may be beneficial. These are sprayed directly on to the leaves, where they are quickly absorbed and show almost instant effects. These are usually used as a pick-me-up for plants that are looking a bit sorry for themselves and in need of a tonic. Foliar feeds are not suitable for plants with tough, glossy foliage or soft, furry leaves. You should also be careful when spraying in the conservatory near furniture and other decorations.

ONE FOR THE POT

A vigorously healthy plant in the specialised conditions of the conservatory is sooner or later going to require potting-on. You will soon recognise a pot-bound plant. Growth slows down despite giving it ideal light, warmth and food; sometimes roots will be visible protruding from the drainage hole. To check, tip the plant, complete with root ball, gently out of the pot (it is best not to do this just after you have watered it). To minimise damage to the plant, cover the surface of the pot with your hand, threading the main stem through your fingers to support the foliage. Turn the pot upside-down and tap the rim gently on a hard surface or with the handle of your trowel; the whole thing should fall neatly away from the pot. You should never try to pull the plant out by its stem. To remove an awkward or prickly plant like a cactus, wrap a soft but protective collar around it, using folded newspaper or one of those padded kitchen cloths to protect the hand when turning out. If the plant is pot-bound, the roots will be thickly matted with very little compost remaining. This a good opportunity to check the condition of the roots, removing any that are dead; look out also for bugs and grubs.

A few plants like to be slightly pot-bound (those with fleshy roots such as clivias, or bulbs like hippeastrums), but for most species you will need to pot-on to encourage it to thrive further. For this you will require a new container allowing no more than 4cm/1.5in of extra space for new

Fig 94 Yucca elephantipes *variegata*.

root growth. Resist the temptation to put your plant in the biggest pot you can find thinking that you will save time when it next needs potting-on, as plants prefer the minimum comfortable size that still allows space for the roots to grow.

Large specimen perennials in the conservatory cannot be potted-on forever, and replacing the top couple of inches of soil with new compost every year will not always keep them in prime condition. According to how vigorously the particular plants like to grow, they may require repotting every year or so. This involves removing the plant from its pot and reducing the size of the root ball by trimming away any old or damaged roots and pulling off excess potting compost. To remove a plant from a large pot, lay it on its side and tap the rim with a wooden mallet or block to loosen it, or use a blade of a long thin knife round the inside edge of the pot. If the pot is heavy, get someone to support the plant while you pull it away. If this fails, you will have to break the pot as gently as possible, or cut

it away if it is a plastic one. Plants should then be replaced in a pot of the same size filled with new potting mixture. Water well to ensure the new compost is moist, but not so much that it becomes waterlogged. The best time to repot a mature plant is after a rest period and before it begins a new season of growth. Do not try to repot or pot-on during a rest phase, or the plant may not be active enough to make adequate new root growth.

Hanging and wall-mounted baskets need to be prepared in the correct manner before adding soil and plants. They need replanting fairly regularly, as soil becomes tired through frequent watering or the liner comes to the end of its useful life. The ideal material for lining is sphagnum moss, and this can often be transferred to the new container if it is still in good condition. The alternative is to use plastic sheeting or preformed sponge-like liners which do not generally last more than twelve months.

Plants in hanging baskets should regularly be trimmed and pruned of any dead material to keep them looking good, but treat the repotting exercise as a good opportunity to make a thorough check of your plant's state of health. Roots may need easing away from the plant liner with as little damage as possible. Line your basket with sphagnum moss, horticultural grade plastic or a preformed liner as appropriate. Make small drainage holes in the bottom of the lining but do not add any crocks. The liner is now filled one-third with potting compost, and slits made in the side of the liner, large enough for the root ball of appropriate trailing plants to be inserted. After pushing in the trailing plants, more compost is added to the basket to cover the roots and the process is repeated until the container is full. A large, mature plant confined to its own hanging basket will have to be top-planted in the usual way, making sure it sits well down in the container for stability. Wall-mounted baskets are planted only on exposed faces, of course. Once the baskets are completed, they should be totally immersed in a bucket of water then drained before hanging up.

Fig 95 Planting a hanging basket. (a) Wire baskets should be lined with moss, plastic sheeting or a synthetic liner to help retain moisture. (b) Add sufficient compost to cover the roots of plants. A peat-based mixture is best for holding moisture and should be damp but not water-saturated. (c) The root ball or cutting is gently inserted between the wire in the lower part of the basket. Add compost to cover the roots.

You can use any type of container for potting-on or repotting providing it is the correct size and has proper drainage. Plain or decorative clay pots look particularly attractive in the conservatory and are available in a wide choice of sizes, shapes and styles. However, plastic pots are lighter and more sturdy, easy to clean, and supplied in a choice of shapes and colours. Because unglazed clay pots are porous they need watering more frequently than plastic ones. Whichever you choose, it must be cleaned thoroughly, clay pots being soaked in fresh water overnight.

Unless the pot is going to be placed on some form of automatic watering tray or platform,

cover the drainage holes with a good layer of stones or broken pieces of pot to encourage good drainage. Add a layer of appropriate moist potting mixture, then ease your plant gently into position, taking care not to damage roots or foliage. Try to get its final position as central and straight as possible; the final level of the top of the compost should be a little below the top of the pot to aid watering. Pack round gently with the potting mixture, making sure you do not cover the lower stems or leaves or that there are no air pockets. You should only exert enough pressure for the soil to hold the plant in position; if you press down too hard, it is in danger of becoming compacted and impeding drainage. Soil-based mixtures can be packed down more firmly than peat-based ones. To settle the compost, tap the pot a couple of times firmly on a hard surface.

Getting the Right Mix

Potting-on and repotting are an excellent way of supplying your plants with new, nutrient-rich compost which will keep them flourishing for the next few months without the need for feeding. Never use soil straight out of the garden – use a specially prepared potting mixture which contains a balanced blend of elements, is sterilised to kill any pests and diseases and which has been specially formulated to allow free drainage, yet holds moisture without becoming waterlogged. However, even within the vast range of proprietary potting mixtures available, some perform better than others according to content; others have been specially formulated to suit a particular plant type with specific needs such as cacti or orchids. Calcifuges or lime-haters such as camellia and heathers will require a special acidic lime-free mix.

Proprietary mixtures tend to be either soil- or peat-based; the soil-based tend to be expensive as their base is sterilised loam, but they perform better, providing a superior store of plant nutrients and holding moisture well. The familiar John Innes mixtures are carefully formulated to suit plants' needs exactly and differ only in the proportion of chalk and fertiliser they contain. John Innes No. I suits slow-growing plants; vigorous annuals, fruits and vegetables will flourish in No. 3 and No. 4, for example. No. 2 is the general purpose mixture, although a great many house plants will do well with John Innes No. 3. You can make your own by mixing seven parts volume sterilised loam with three parts peat and two parts washed coarse sand. For No. I, add to each 36 litres/8 gallons (around 1.25 cubic feet) 113g/4oz of John Innes base fertiliser and 21g/¾oz of powdered chalk (unless making up a mixture for lime-hating plants). Double the quantities of base fertiliser and chalk to make John Innes No. 2, treble them for No. 3, and so on. The base fertiliser which can be bought ready mixed is two parts hoof and horn to an eighth inch grist (13 per cent nitrogen), two parts calcium phosphate (18 per cent phosphoric acid) and one part potassium sulphate (48 per cent potash) – all parts by weight. Alternatively, John Innes mixtures are widely available ready mixed, but quality varies widely so choose a reputable make.

Peat-based, soilless composts are less expensive and do not use loam, but are made up of equal parts by volume of peat and washed sand or grit to make a general purpose mixture. Some are based entirely on peat, which are good for acid-loving plants such as azaleas. Others include perlite and vermiculite instead of sand to improve moisture retention and aeration. The addition of sand or grit increases the weight of your plant container, making it more stable and

Fig 96   Azalea simsii.

95

Fig 97 Spathiphyllum '*Supreme*'.

haters. When using peat to make up a potting mixture it should be fairly moist, but the sand should be dry for mixing. The disadvantage of peat-based potting composts is that they must never be allowed to dry out, particularly when plants are growing in them, as they are difficult to re-hydrate.

It is not just lime-hating plants that need special consideration when it comes to their growing medium. Other plant groups also have special needs, and supplying them with the ideal potting mixture, or as near to it as you can get, will increase your chances of success. Proprietary mixtures for cacti and orchids are available from garden centres and specialist suppliers, for example, or you can make up your own. Compost for orchids contains a high percentage of fir bark chippings, to be as close as possible to their natural food source. The bark alone makes a perfectly adequate medium for growing epiphytic or desert orchids (terrestrial orchids will tolerate more ordinary mixtures providing they are very porous) since it is well draining, slow to rot and easy to work with, although it will require additional fertiliser as recommended for orchids.

The correct soil mix for cacti, by contrast, must include grit or sharp sand to encourage good drainage and aeration; complete and constant drainage is essential. Soilless composts for cacti, for example, should contain at least 30 per cent volume small, sharp washed grit. You could add grit to a proprietary brand or to a John Innes mixture if you prefer soil-based compost. Alternatively mix up your own using one part sterilised loam to one part well-sifted decomposed leaf mould and one part sharp, washed grit or sand plus a little slow-release fertiliser.

improving drainage. Ready-mixed mineral combinations are available for adding to your own peat mixtures, or you can make up your own by adding to every 36 litres/8 gallons, 85g/3oz of ammonium nitrate, 28g/1oz of potassium sulphate, 85g/3oz of hoof and horn, 57g/2oz of magnesium limestone (dolomite),. 113g/4oz of chalk and 57g/2oz of calcium superphosphate. Omit the chalk if making up compost for lime

CHAPTER 5

Plant Health and Disease

CHECK LIST

If you are not giving your conservatory plants the correct light, heat, humidity, food or water, they will soon let you know by looking off-colour and wilting or drooping. Keep an eye open for tell-tale signs so that they can be promptly remedied; caught in the early stages, most ailments can be treated with complete recovery. Allow them to get worse and your plant will die.

Slow Growth

If the plant is not in one of its resting periods, slow growth may indicate that it needs potting-on. If you find it is not pot-bound, perhaps it needs a good feed or more light; overwatering will also retard growth so check if the compost is too wet. Poor growth combined with pale and sparse foliage usually indicates too much warmth, moisture or fertiliser during a time when the plant should be resting.

Wilting

If you suspect heat or light levels are too high or you have been neglecting your watering duties, water immediately (if the compost has dried out and shrunk away from the pot, *see* remedial action on page 85) and spray the leaves. If this does not revive it, there is something wrong with the roots, usually rotting due to overwatering or pest infestation. Sometimes overfeeding damages the roots with a build-up of salts. If you know you have been watering your plant correctly and

nothing else seems wrong, move to a cooler, shadier position.

Leaf Drop

Shock is the most common cause of leaves, buds and flowers dropping off your plants. This might be due to a sudden change of light or temperature, but overwatering or overfeeding could have the same effect. Providing the reaction is not too severe, you will simply have to nurse the plant back to health by taking special care to provide ideal, constant conditions.

Yellowing Leaves

The occasional lower leaf will turn yellow and drop off, but if the whole plant starts looking a bit pale and sickly, it has probably caught a chill or is suffering from overwatering or an over-dry atmosphere. Check for draughts and humidity or ease off on the watering. Poor colour is sometimes an indication of lack of nutrients, probably nitrogen or sometimes magnesium; in lime-hating plants it indicates too alkaline a potting mixture, or hard water.

Brown Patches

If there is no indication of fungal disease and the leaves are turning brown or developing brown patches, check that you have not been overfeeding or that the plant is not suffering from a potash deficiency. Another cause is burning from sudden chill or frost, or from intense sunlight.

Fig 98   Leaf yellowing.

Accidentally splashing the leaves with liquid fertiliser or pesticide, or exposing the plant to fumes from unsuitable heaters or poisonous wood preservatives, will also create brown patches.

No Flowers

If a flowering plant fails to produce blooms, check that it is not a species that requires special conditions like a period of drought (as for African Violets), slightly pot-bound roots or a period of complete dark before flowering. Some plants have to reach a certain stage of maturity before they will bloom. If nature has no reason for it, and the plant seems to have produced a lot of foliage, you have been feeding it too much. Ease off the fertiliser, prune or repot in smaller pot. Sometimes the level of heat is wrong, so double-check whether you plant is getting too little or too much. *See also* leaf drop (page 97) for plants whose buds fall off before they get a chance to flower.

Rotting

Over-enthusiastic watering is the commonest cause of plants rotting and keeling over, particularly in cold weather. Take special care during the winter months if your conservatory is not being heated, and especially if plants are resting, when they will require less moisture in any case.

Withered Leaf Tips

An over-dry atmosphere may cause leaf edges to wither; this is also caused by people brushing past the plant on a regular basis, or maybe fluoride in the water you are using. Mist spraying or repositioning the plant may help. Cut off the damaged tips where possible.

Loss of Variegation

If a variegated plant starts to turn green it is either reverting to type or receiving too little light. Cut out reverted shoots or improve light requirement.

Rosette Rot

If a rosette-forming plant rots in the centre, it often means water has been standing there or that conditions are too cold. The plant will have to be destroyed; take care not to overwater next time.

Unhealthy Roots

Soft roots, maybe ones which are even starting to go rotten, indicate that your potting mixture is too wet or that the plant is overfed. Repot and provide humid conditions while re-rooting. Dried up roots mean you have not watered enough; soak the pot thoroughly, draining well when compost and roots are moist again.

PLANT HEALTH

In the enclosed, self-contained environment of the conservatory, mischief-making insects and debilitating diseases likely to affect your plants do not occur naturally. But however careful you are, bugs may be brought in from outside on a new plant or make their way in from the garden. Diseases such as fungus or mildew can develop through poor ventilation, or incorrect balance of humidity and temperature within the conservatory, or be picked up by a plant that has been placed outside for any reason. Some infestation is inevitable and this is why it is important to maintain both conservatory and plants in the best of health, as described in the previous section.

The best form of control is not to allow the problem near your plants in the first place. New plants should be inspected thoroughly for any sign of sickness or pests; temporary flowering plants seem particularly prone to infestation. It may be worth keeping a new plant in quarantine for a week or so to see if anything develops before putting it with the others.

It also helps to be as clean and tidy as possible, removing dead material and clearing up any spills of soil or water. Remove fallen leaves and faded flowers as soon as you see them. Pots, glass, shelves and general surroundings should also be kept clean and tidy, and sterilised at least once or twice a year. Regular washing or misting of leaves on foliage plants with a mild soapy solution is a good preventative measure and the leaf joints and stems are worth examining at the same time for any sign of pest infestation. Eggs may be tiny but these inaccessible places are exactly where they like to be laid. Prompt action will not only help prevent problems taking hold or even maybe developing in the first place; cleanliness, the right conditions and adequate feeding will also improve plants' resistance.

Cramped roots encourage rot and damp; unventilated conditions may lead to mildew; but clean leaves are less likely to collect fungal spores than dirty ones. Plants put outside during the summer seem most at risk from pests or fungus and it may be advisable to spray these with a mild fungicide before bringing them back into the conservatory. Should a problem occur, it is important to eradicate it as swiftly as possible since those very conditions that protect plants in the conservatory from widespread exposure to such perils in the garden will provide a perfect breeding place once a colony or disease takes hold. If you see a plant looking below par or showing tell-tale signs, remove it immediately and give it your close attention before the problem can spread to its companions. Early treatment also means that you can use less drastic measures. It should be remembered that pesticides are poisonous and ought to be employed as little as possible, particularly since many conservatory pests are showing signs of resistance through over-enthusiastic use.

Obviously, prevention is better than cure, but some problems are bound to occur and you must keep your head, taking the time to choose exactly the right treatment and checking the instructions closely to make sure that you are not only using it correctly but that it is suitable for your particular plant. Some pesticides will damage certain plants and hopefully those at risk will be listed on the container. These include: malathion, which should never be used on ferns, petunias or pileas; azobenzene which will damage young plants and those in flower as well as selected foliage species; or dimethoate, harmful to fuchsias, primulas, hydrangeas and various other flowering species. Many pesticides can also injure pets such as fish, caged birds or small mammals, and even young children. Always keep pesticides in a locked cupboard in well-labelled containers, and wear gloves when handling them yourself, particularly when spraying.

Pesticide sprays are particularly hazardous and you should consider wearing a face mask when using one. Take the plant outside to spray whenever possible, or protect neighbouring plants with a piece of paper. A small manual pump-action sprayer is preferable to an aerosol and you should take care not to spray too close or you may damage the leaves. Spraying is one way of tackling the problem, and is probably the swiftest and most efficient; make sure it is applied as a fine mist and remember to treat the undersides of leaves as well as the top surface. An alternative for small plants is to immerse stems and leaves in a bath of diluted pesticide, wearing rubber gloves.

Pesticide is also available as a dust which is less effective but causes less damage should you have to treat plants with open blooms. Small infestations may be satisfactorily treated with a small, stiff artists' paint brush dipped in methylated spirit or an insecticide solution. Another method is the use of pesticidal granules sprinkled on the surface of the soil, or sticks which are pushed into it. The chemicals are released by watering, to be absorbed by the roots, protecting the upper parts of the plant by systemic action. These have a slower but more long term effect than sprays. Serious infestation may mean the conservatory has to be fumigated and this is best done in the evening when the fumes can be left overnight to carry on their work. Sealing any cracks around

doors and window frames with wet sacking or similar will prevent fumes from escaping into the house. The conservatory should be well ventilated the next morning. You will have to calculate the total volume of your conservatory to know exactly how much fumigant to purchase and remove any furniture and furnishings.

Always make the chemical solution your last resort; early treatment may allow less stringent measures. Large pests can often be removed with your fingers or tweezers and smaller ones swabbed away with a piece of cotton wool soaked in methylated spirit, alcohol or a soap solution. When using chemicals, do make sure you follow the instructions to the letter.

Popular Pesticides

There are a great many chemicals readily available to treat plant problems, often sold under different proprietery names. Sometimes several chemicals are combined to create a certain pesticide. Do not use one particular product for any length of time as pests tend to build up a resistance. Always double-check instructions before using and take the appropriate protective measures. The following names may be familiar and common remedies. Fungicide chemicals tend to be less toxic to mammals than pesticides, but still need cautious handling.

Butoxicarboxim is the systemic element in plant sticks for killing mites.
Benomyl is systemic and effective against a wide range of fungal diseases.
Derris is a natural plant product effective against aphids and mites but harmful to fish.
Dimethoate is the most widely used systemic but cannot be used for mite infestation.
Malathion is an all-purpose pesticide which seems to kill virtually every kind of pest.
Pirimophos-methyl kills a wide range of pests, especially whitefly and mites, but is ineffective against scale insect or mealy bug.
Pyrethrum is a safe, plant-based pesticide, safer to use if you have pets.

Fig 99 A smoke cone.

Resmethrin is a synthetic treatment, very like Pyrethrum and again safe to use if you have pets.
Streptomycin is an antibiotic used to control bacterial disease.
Sulphur dust is a traditional and effective treatment for rot.
Thiophanate-methyl is a systemic pesticide effective against a wide range of fungus diseases.

PLANT DISEASES

The majority of plant diseases likely to attack conservatory plants are fungal ones, brought on by poor conditions, particularly excess moisture combined with cold. Plants may also be affected by a viral disease usually spread by insects and causing stunted growth, discoloured leaves and distortion: there is no cure for viral diseases and afflicted plants should be removed and destroyed as soon as possible.

Blackleg attacks cuttings of fleshy plants such as pelargoniums, but can also spread to mature plants. It is caused by overwatering or saturated compost. Make cuttings of unaffected top growth and destroy the remaining plant.
Botrytis or grey mould is a fungus officially known as *Botrytis cinerea*, a particular nuisance amongst conservatory plants. It is identified by its fluffy, grey appearance, like furry mould. If you disturb an affected plant, clouds of fine dust which are the spores, rise from it. The spores are always present in the air and attack plants when the air is too humid, particularly in cool conditions. Avoid over-enthusiastic mist spraying. Remove affected parts and apply a fungicide.
Leaf spot covers foliage with different sized blister-like spots of brown, yellow or white. They result from fungi or bacteria and are encouraged by allowing water droplets to remain on foliage. Remove affected leaves and spray with fungicide.
Mildew is easily identified by the white, powder-like mould it produces on leaves, stems and flowers. Soft-leaved plants like begonias are most at risk in the conservatory, as are fruit trees and

Fig 100 Botrytis.

bushes. It can be difficult to prevent infestation even using fungicides in a cool conservatory, especially where plants are crowded close together. Overwatering and poor ventilation do not help. There are some proprietary fungicides which are good for controlling mildew.
Rusts produce red brown spots on many plants, particularly pelargoniums and should be treated with a dithane spray as soon as the symptoms are seen.
Sooty mould appears after infestation of sap-sucking insects like aphid and scale, growing on the glistening 'honeydew' and looking like black mould. Fungicidal sprays may kill it but the un-sightly mould remains so you are advised to remove it manually with a soft cloth dipped in soapy water or the appropriate fungicide solution.

PLANT PESTS

Pest control can be difficult in conservatories used as living areas, since widescale sprays and fumigants are not ideal. Hopefully, the problem will be minimal and local, so controlled spraying

Fig 101   Aphids.

Fig 102   Greenfly.

will be adequate for a large variety of pests such as greenfly, red spider mites, whitefly, scale and thrips. If you prefer not to use chemicals, you might like to try a form of biological control ideally suited to the enclosed conditions of a conservatory. Parasitic insects guaranteed to keep whitefly and red spider mite under control are available from specialist suppliers (by post). The best time to introduce them into the conservatory is in early to mid spring. Predators can only be used if you are already suffering from the pests, otherwise they will have nothing to feed on. You will also not be able to use fungicides if you are employing biological controls.

Ants can sometimes invade the conservatory from outdoors and while they themselves do not harm the plants, they have an infuriating habit of carrying aphids from one plant to another. They may also disturb plant roots with their tunnelling. Treat with proprietery ant bait.

Aphids also known as plant lice or greenfly, can also be brown, pink, grey or black. They are one of the commonest plant pests, and some plants seem more prone to attack than others. Aphids like new, soft growth and suck the plant's sap, causing poor growth and yellow, distorted leaves.

Almost any plant seems prone, except bromeliads. The sticky deposit they produce, called honeydew, prevents leaves functioning properly and attracts sooty mould. Wash off with soapy water followed by a clear water rinse; or spray with malathion.

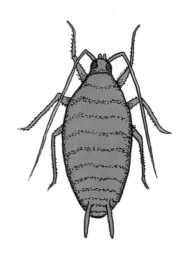

Fig 103   A single greenfly.

Caterpillars, the larvae of butterflies and moths, can virtually destroy a plant very quickly by eating the leaves. Pick them off by hand or spray with liquid derris.

Cyclamen mites are a common pest and difficult to spot, affecting a wide range of indoor plants. Symptoms are stunted leaves and flowers, sometimes distortion and curling of leaf edges. They can be difficult to control safely and it may be better to destroy affected plants.

Earwigs eat holes in petals and leaves at night. Flowers can be dusted or ant bait put down near to cracks and holes which are the likely daytime lairs of earwigs.

Mealy bugs look like small, pink woodlice, usually hidden in a coat of grey-white wool. They gather in the angle between leaf stalk and stem and particularly like cacti and succulents. Swab them with cotton wool soaked in methylated spirit or surgical spirit, or use a paint brush dipped in insecticide solution.

Red spider mite can only just be seen with the naked eye but their effects are easily identified in the shape of yellow mottled leaves which eventually go brown and shrivel, and a fine white web covering the underside of leaves. These pests are

Fig 105   Red spider mite web.

the scourge of hot, dry conservatories and will punish plants who really prefer cooler conditions. Liquid derris or malathion can be effective; you may have to repeat spray after three days and again after ten days. Badly infested leaves and stems should be cut off. Widespread infestation may have to be fumigated with azobenzene. Regular mist spraying may help to prevent problems.

Root mealy bugs are similar to mealy bugs but attack the root systems of plants, especially succulents. You may see white patches or specks of wool on roots when repotting. Drench the potting mixture with pesticide, preferably a systemic type, and sterilise pots before reuse.

Scale insects look like miniature limpets and suck the sap of plants. There are many variations, some specific to a particular species, and some plants such as citrus and oleander are specially susceptible. They must be rubbed off manually with a soft cloth dipped in soapy water or pesticide solution and all crevices treated with a small paint brush. Regular use of a systemic pesticide will help prevent an attack and is less time-consuming.

Sciarid-fly maggots, sometimes called fungus gnats, look like small, black-headed worms. They

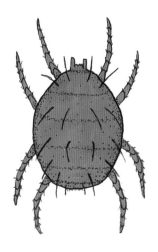

Fig 104   A red spider mite.

eat plant roots and thrive in damp, humid conditions. They hatch into gnats which may be killed with fly-killer to prevent them laying eggs; kill the maggots by watering the potting mixture with malathion.

Slugs, also snails and woodlice, often escape from the garden into the conservatory and can do considerable damage by eating foliage or, in the case of woodlice, the roots. Use proprietary slug and snail bait or pick off by hand if the infestation is not widespread. Woodlice can be controlled by BHC powders.

Thrips produce white patches surrounded by small black specks on the leaves and are tiny black winged insects which will drop out on to a sheet of white paper if the plant is shaken. Use a systemic insecticide or a malathion or derris spray.

Weevils will attack pot plants like primulas, cyclamen and succulents. The curved white grubs will completely demolish plant roots, causing it to collapse. The adults look like a beetle with a long proboscis. An infested plant will probably be beyond saving, although adding an appropriate insecticide to the potting compost may help prevent attack in prone plants.

Whitefly are the clouds of tiny white insects which rise up *en masse* when an affected plant is disturbed. They can be a particular problem in conservatories, especially on flowering plants. The larvae are sap-sucking and produce honeydew, turning leaves yellow. The larvae are immune to pesticides, so eradication can be difficult. Repeated spraying with malathion and liquid derris may do the trick.

GOING ON HOLIDAY

In your enthusiasm for building up an exciting collection of conservatory plants, spare a thought for how they are going to manage while you are away from home. Even a small collection will be worth a considerable amount of money and probably represent a great deal of time and care, which even a day or so without the correct heat,

humidity and water requirements could ruin completely. You must consider how your conservatory will be looked after while you are away on holiday or if you work away from home for extended periods. Also bear in mind that a glasshouse attached to your home may represent a security risk, and getting someone to look after your plants will also be useful for keeping an eye on things generally. Good locks should be fixed to both indoor and outdoor doors, and ventilation should be of the type that can be fixed at a burglar-proof crack of an opening.

The problem is usually finding someone with the experience and concern to take over the rather specialised needs of a conservatory. A well-meaning but poorly briefed neighbour could destroy your plants simply by overwatering or allowing the conservatory to become too cold or too hot. Of course, many plant requirements in the conservatory can be handled automatically. If you know you are going to be away a lot of the time, particularly during the colder months, you should consider a heating system with automatic and thermostatic control as outlined in Chapter 2. There are also automatic ventilation systems which are worth installing anyway to cope with temperature fluctuations while you are out during the day. The best way to cope with shading is to pull shades down before you go, unless you have a collection of plants with specialist light needs – in which case artificial lighting systems can also be operated on automatic timers. If you are going away for a long time during the winter when light is limited but shading is still sometimes required, then you will have to come to some arrangment with a near-neighbour.

Watering is going to be your main concern. There are a variety of automatic watering methods, some of which have been described already on page 84, although these systems are usually only suitable for clay and not plastic pots. As a temporary measure, a length of bandage, lampwick, proprietary plant-pot wick or 2.5cm/ 1 in strips of capillary matting with one end in a bowl of water and the other pushed into the soil will draw up water by capillary action. Alterna-

Fig 106   Take precautions when going on holiday, otherwise your plants may suffer.

tively, insert your wick through the drainage hole of your pot to about 7.5cm/3in (you may have to use a stick) and stand the pot in water or on a tray of damp stones or gravel. You can also buy porous containers which are inserted into the soil next to the plant and will release water gradually over a period of two to three weeks.

Placing plants in plastic bags fastened at the top with a tie or rubber band encloses it in its own little atmosphere maintaining good humidity and a moist soil for around two weeks. Three or four thin stakes or sticks pushed into the compost will hold the bag clear of plant foliage. This is only suitable for plants in shadier positions and it may be worth moving all bar real sun-lovers into a shadier spot before you go away or out of strong light into temperatures of between 16–18°C/ 60–65°F. You can buy a special plastic plant dome which works on the same principal as a polythene bag but which stands rigid like a miniature tent, usually about 90cm/36in high and 74cm/29in across – big enough to take several quite large plants and keep them in good condition for at least a fortnight.

Mulching large plants and those in beds with peat or stones is useful to slow down moisture evaporation. In winter, pack damp peat around plant pots. Unfortunately, unless you have a very sophisticated automatic system, plants with very special needs will have to rely on the kind attentions of a friend or neighbour. It may be a good idea to keep a detailed diary of exactly the tasks you have to maintain in the conservatory during one week, which can be passed on to your willing stand-in as a guide.

Just before you go, water plants as required, cut away any foliage that looks in poor condition, double-check for pests or diseases and remove any flowers or buds that are about to open.

CHAPTER 6

Plant Listing

INTERESTING FOLIAGE PLANTS

An interesting selection of foliage plants is essential for your conservatory to be successful. The simple effect of different shades of green creates that lush, jungle effect so loved by the Victorians. The vast range of exotic foliage shapes available from swords and blades to heart and arrow shapes offer plenty of exciting opportunities for contrasts. With the options among variegated cultivars providing spots, stripes and splashes of red, purple, cream, silver and gold, you hardly need showy flowers at all, save to add highlights at certain points through the season.

Many of your familiar house plants will do well in the conservatory, growing anywhere up to twice their previous size. However, the majority prefer high humidity and will need regular spraying. You will also find that most foliage plants do not enjoy direct sunlight, so reserve for them the lower shelves of your staging or the shadier corners. The conservatory offers a good chance to grow some of the more temperamental species that will thrive in the warmth, providing you keep them well watered.

Aglaonema (Chinese Evergreen) 60cm/2ft. Makes an attractive clump of leathery leaves, usually variegated. *A. crispum* is silver with dark green streaks.

Caladium 60cm/2ft. Large, arrow-shaped leaves come in a choice of reds, green, creams and pinks. Needs to overwinter in a dark corner.

Chamaerops humilis (European Fan Palm) 1.2m/4ft. Attractive fan-shaped leaves on tall stalks. It likes plenty of light but a cool spot in winter. Water well in summer.

Chrysalidocarpus lutescens (The Butterfly Palm) 2.5–6m/8–20ft. Needs a humid atmosphere, but enjoys warm conditions. Ideal day temperature is around 24–29°C (75–84°F), and a night temperature of 16°C (60°F). Very pretty delicate foliage.

Coffee arabica (Arabian Coffee Plant) 2m/6ft.

Fig 107 Pleomele reflexa *'Variegata'.*

Enjoys warmth, but needs shade and good ventilation. Coppery foliage turns dark green and is followed by small, white fragrant flowers and red berries.

Coleus blumei lm/3ft. Fleshy leaves in a choice of strong colour combinations, mainly reds, greens and creams.

Cordyline terminalis (Cabbage Palm) 60cm/2ft. Has glossy tongue-like leaves in dark greens and reds. *C. terminalis* 'Firebrand' has red edges; 'Tricolour' has pink, cream and green foliage.

Dieffenbachia (Dumb Cane) 2m/6ft. This slow-growing tropical shrub likes a humid atmosphere. The robust *D. amoena* has white and yellow markings; *D. bowmanni* is the largest with dark green leaves up to 75cm/30in long.

Dizygotheca elegantissima (False Aralia) 1.8m/6ft. A graceful plant with very narrow, bootlace leaves which are a dark coppery red colour, sometimes almost black. Prefers warm but humid conditions.

Dracaena 60–100cm/2–3ft. A palm-like foliage plant with elegant, striped, sword-shaped leaves. It likes light and warmth but should be protected from direct sunshine. *D. godseffiana* is speckled with yellow like gold-dust; *D. deremensis* 'Warneckii' has pointed leaves striped grey, green and silver; *D. fragrans* has broader leaves with gold and green stripes; *D. marginata* is almost grass-like with very narrow pink, cream and green leaves.

Episcia cupreata Creeper. A trailing evergreen with soft, furry foliage marked red and silver. Good for use in hanging baskets. Will produce tiny red flowers.

Fittonia 8–10cm/3–4in. A low-growing plant with interesting rounded leaves strongly marked with white, pink or red veining. Likes humidity.

Fig 108 Dieffenbachia *'Tropic Snow'.*

Gynura aurantiaca (Velvet Plant) lm/3ft. The long, pointed leaves are covered in purple hairs, giving this plant an appearance rather like purple velvet. Can be trained along wires.

Howeia 2m/6ft. A palm which must be kept shady but which tolerates heat and doesn't need much moisture, and so is good for a shady or under-shelf position. It has the typical arching fronds associated with palms and is very elegant.

Neoregelia 30–60cm/12–24in. A Bromeliad requiring good light but not direct sunlight. It makes a dense rosette of attractive foliage, depending on species. The flowers are a bonus – and tend to affect the coloration of the leaves. For example, *N. carolinae* has shiny green leaves and produces purple flowers with red/purple bracts; *N. carolinae* 'Tricolor' has white-striped leaves which go red when the flowers appear. *N. spectabilis,* which has red-tipped leaves, turns

Fig 109 Neoregelia carolinae.

completely red in the centre when the blue flowers appear.

Olea europae (Olive) 4.5m/15ft. Interesting, often contorted trunk supports small leathery grey leaves. Fruits when mature.

Pandanus (Screw Pine) 1–2m/3–6ft. A large plant with arching leaves from a central stem. The largest is *P. utilis*, which has dark green leaves edged with red spines. Smaller is *P. sanderi* which has narrower, pale green leaves striped white; or *P. veitchii*, whose foliage is dark green with a wide yellow stripe. The plant requires good light but not direct sunlight.

Plectranthus 1m/3ft. A pretty trailing evergreen with attractive foliage and winter flowers. It likes light but is only really suited to cool conservatories as it needs moderate temperatures. *P. coleoides* 'Marginatus' is particularly pretty if you have the right conditions, producing fresh green foliage with white markings.

Rhapis excelsa 1.2–2m/4–6ft. An exotic-looking dwarf palm with leathery veined leaves on stiff stalks. Prefers cool conditions in winter of around 7°C (45°F).

Palms

We think of palms as traditional conservatory plants but in fact, although they like plenty of sunshine, they only thrive in damp, humid conditions. We have mentioned a few which are perhaps a little more tolerant, providing they are kept moist. Should you be prepared to maintain a humid atmosphere in the conservatory, you could grow a wider choice. There are plants which look like graceful palms but are in fact more tolerant, and we have already included some of these above – *Cordyline*, *Dracaena* and *Pandanus*. You are unlikely to be able to grow the *Kentia* palms in a conservatory since they abhor hot, dry conditions.

Chamaedorea elegans 1.2m/4ft. A dwarf palm with long, feathery fronds.

Cocos weddeliana (Coconut Palm) 50cm/18in. Dwarf form of the coconut palm, with feathery leaflets.

Neanthe bella 50cm/18in. Useful dwarf palm which tolerates a dry atmosphere.

Phoenix dactylifera (Date Palm) 15m/49ft. The slow-growing Date Palm with its prickly leaves should not out-grow the room for 10–15 years. There is a dwarf form, *P. roebelinii*, which has graceful, shiny, dark green pinnate leaves with sharp spines at the base. This grows to no more than 150cm/5ft.

Rheinhardtia gracilis (Window Palm) 150cm/5ft. Dwarf palm with attractive long-stemmed fronds.

Ferns

Like palms, ferns seem to offer exactly the right kind of exotic, feathery foliage expected in a lush conservatory. However, conditions are again frequently less than ideal; ferns like a cool, moist atmosphere and the only way to grow any but the tougher types is to create a specialist fern conservatory or a cool area within a larger one, where you will find planting a collection of ferns close together in a trough or special bed helps increase the level of moisture and humidity around the plants. A north-facing conservatory would be a good candidate; packing the spaces between the plants with damp peat or moss will also prevent too much moisture loss. Ferns come in a wonderful variety of forms, and are superb in contrasting groups, or when grown as single specimens in hanging baskets or trailing down pillars. Positioning plants around a small pool or fountain within the conservatory provides a more humid atmosphere and may suit some of the more tolerant fern species.

Adiantum (Maidenhair Fern) 60cm/2ft. Makes a dense mass of arching light green fronds of tiny leaflets on slender, wiry stems. Likes shade but tolerates warmth in summer.

Asplenium (Spleenwort) 60cm–1.2m/2–4ft. An attractive fern with lacy green fronds. The Bird's-nest Fern, *A. nidus*, is unusual in that it has undivided glossy leaves almost like tongues.

Blechnum gibbum 1m/3ft. A tropical fern which forms a dense crown of well-defined green fronds.

Cyrtomium falcatum 30–60cm/1–2ft. Makes a loose arrangement of glossy evergreen fronds on woody stems. Unusually, it will withstand dry air and draughts.

Davallia canariensis (Hare's-foot Fern) 30–45cm/12–18in. Makes a mass of delicate but tough feathery fronds.

Didymochlaena truncatula 45cm/18in. An unusual fern with tall, open fronds of yellow/green turning very dark green as they mature.

Nephrolepis exalta (Sword Fern) 1m/3ft. A good fern for hanging baskets or to position on top of a classical pillar, making a tall plant with dense green fronds. Most popular is *N. exalta* 'Bostoniensis', The Boston Fern, which has a cascading habit.

Pellaea rotundifolia 20cm/8in. Round leaves strung like beads along reddish wiry stems. Enjoys good light and warmth and can be watered normally.

Platycerium (Staghorn Fern) 1m/3ft. A strange-looking plant, with leaves like green antlers, usually grown attached to a log or branch. Must not be allowed to dry out.

Pteris (Brake) 1.2m/4ft. Beautiful lacy fronds on reddish stems.

Selaginalla (Creeping Moss) 10–45cm/4–18in. Both creeping and erect forms have attractive moss-like foliage.

CLIMBERS AND TWINERS

Climbing plants or creepers and twiners, that can be trained up canes or along wires, are very important in the conservatory. They add height and interest, softening the structure and in many cases filtering strong sunlight to the advantage of other plants. Many offer the bonus of spectacular exotic blooms at certain times of the year and it is worth planning a few of these for seasonal highlights. Several species grow fast, producing a pleasing effect within a single season – there is an exciting choice of foliage shape and colours too. Plants can be grown in direct beds or in containers, and should be supported by wires (which will be near-invisible on the walls), or sometimes by trellises erected where appropriate.

[C] denotes a climber suited to cooler conservatories.

Abutilon (Flowering Maple) A tropical evergreen shrub with maple-shaped leaves. It is not, strictly speaking, a climber but it can be trained along wires. Hybrids produce bell-shaped flowers in shades of orange, yellow or purple.

Allamanda (Golden Trumpet) With pointed shiny leaves and lovely large yellow flowers, this plant can reach 6m/19ft. *A. cathartica* 'Grandiflora' has particularly lovely flowers, 8cm/3in across.

Ampelopsis [C] A member of the vine family, tolerant of warm dry conditions, this is a good trailer which does not really like full sun and prefers a cool winter. Sometimes sold as *Vitis*.

Antigon leptopus [C] (Coral Vine) A perennial climber with arrow-shaped leaves which should be trained on wires. Makes clusters of

Fig 110 Abutilon x hybridum *'Souvenir de Bonn'.*

delicate pink flowers and prefers plenty of humidity.

Asparagus falcatus [C] A twining evergreen which makes a bushy plant of delicate foliage.

Asparagus myriocladis [C] Feathery fronds are pretty and delicate.

Asteranthera ovata [C] A trailing creeper producing tubular red-and-white-throated flowers. Prefers semi-shade.

Beaumontia grandiflora (Herald's Trumpet) Large oval leaves and white trumpet flowers.

Bougainvillaea [C] A deciduous climber growing to 4.6–6m/15–20ft and well loved for its purple, pink or orange bracts that make a lovely display throughout summer. Allow to dry out in winter and prune back in late winter to about 2.5cm/1in of the previous year's growth.

Cestrum purpureum Produces hanging clusters of burgundy-coloured flowers.

Chorizema cordatum (Flame Pea) Orange and yellow flowers on delicate stems are borne against prickly heart-shaped leaves.

Cissus antarctica [C] (Kangaroo Vine) A natural climber supporting itself with tendrils and producing a mass of ovate, glossy green leaves. It prefers cool conditions of around 13°C (55°F) and will tend to shrivel in a heated conservatory.

Clianthus puniceus (Parrots Bill) A shrubby evergreen climber from New Zealand producing extraordinary clusters of glistening, spiky, scarlet flowers in early summer. Foliage is delicate and frondy, and needs tying or clipping to a framework before pruning to shape.

Cobaea scandens [C] (Cup and Saucer Vine) An annual and fast-growing climber, although it will overwinter. Flowers late but the plant makes a good temporary filler. Flowers are unusual, shaded cream to purple on a green calyx – good for flower arranging.

Gloriosa rothschildiana [C] (Gloriosa Lily) A tuberous species with exotic deep pink flowers. Dies back in winter.

Hardenbergia monophylla (Coral Pea) A climber that can reach heights of 3m/10ft and produces a mass of mauve and yellow flowers.

Hedera [C] (Ivy) Ivies offer a wonderful range of quick-growing climbers with many foliage types and shades. However, they are only for cool conservatories since warm conditions seem to make them prone to red spider mite. Cooler environments can take advantage of the very attractive *H. helix* 'Buttercup', a slow grower with yellow foliage that tolerates semi-sunshine.

Hoya [C] A vigorous evergreen with fleshy

leaves that makes clusters of star-shaped white flowers. Prefers a humid atmosphere. *H. carnosa* 'Variegata' has pink-edged green leaves; *H. bella* is a dwarf form with pendulous stems which is good for hanging baskets.

Ipomoea [C] (Morning Glory) A popular and vigorous climber with trumpet-like purple flowers and purple stems. Trains well on wires. Some cultivars have red or blue flowers.

Jasminum polyanthum [C] (Jasmine) A fast-growing and vigorous ever-green with delicate ferny leaves, growing a mass of tiny white-scented flowers in late winter.

Lapageria rosea [C] A twiner with pink/red waxy bell-like flowers in summer and autumn. Variety 'Flesh Pink' is exactly that colour and prefers semi-shade.

Mandevilla suaveolens [C] (Chilean Jasmine) Fragrant white summer flowers and bright green heart-shaped leaves. Likes plenty of sun.

Oxypetalum caeruleum Grown for its fragrant blue flowers.

Passiflora [C] (Passion Flower) The Passion Flower is an excellent climber, popular for its spectacular blooms. For cool conservatories the hardiest and most familiar, with eye-catching blue blooms and white markings, is *P. caerulea*. Or choose *P. racemosa*, which has red flowers. A heated conservatory offers the chance to grow more unusual forms – *P. caeruleo-racemosa* is a stunning hybrid with purple flowers and blue-green leaves; fast-growing *P. x caponii* 'John Innes' combines large burgundy blooms with purple and white filaments; the red Passion Flower, *P. coccinea*, has brilliant red flowers with pink and white filaments and oval, toothed leaves.

Philodendron [C] A good foliage plant with glossy green tough leaves. Likes humidity in spring and summer (especially the variegated

Fig III Philodendron 'Imperial Red'.

forms), and grows large. *P. scandens* has heart-shaped leaves; *P. erubescens* has large, coppery coloured leaves with a pink tinge when young.

Pittosporum [C] Excellent tough plant for large conservatories, growing to 2.4m/8ft. The leathery leaves are glossy green. *P. tobira* and *P. undulatum* both do well in cool, well-ventilated conditions. *P. eugeniodes variegatum* makes more of a bush and will tolerate neglect.

Plumbago capensis [C] An evergreen with pretty powder-blue flowers.

Pyrostegea ignea A self-climber with pointed leaves and bright orange-red flowers.

Rhodochiton atrosanguineum (Purple Bell Vine) A perennial, if short-lived, climber with heart-shaped, veined leaves and curious fuchsia-like blooms of red and purple-black. Looks spectacular in full bloom, early summer.

Rhodochiton volubile [C] (Purple Bells) A delicate-looking climber with strange red and purple blooms like exaggerated fuchsia blossom.

Solanum jasminoides [C] A semi-evergreen which likes sun. Slate blue flowers with yellow centres appear in late summer. *S. j. casminoides* 'Album' has white and yellow flowers.

Sollya heterophylla [C] (Bluebell Creeper) Sun-loving twiner which produces clusters of bell-like blue flowers in late summer.

Swainsonia galegifolia Produces purple-red flowers in summer.

Tecomaria capensis [C] A twiner with scarlet trumpet flowers in summer.

Thunbergia [C] (Black-Eyed Susan) Another good-tempered climber and a popular trailer with its mass of orange or yellow flowers with a distinct dark eye against the large, fresh green leaves.

Trachelospermum jasmonoides Glossy dark evergreen with creamy white flowers. *T. asiaticum* is a sun-loving evergreen with fragrant white and yellow flowers. *T. jasmonoides* 'Variegatum' has attractive creamy white splashes on the green foliage.

Tropaeolum tuberosum [C] Related to the bedding nasturtium, this vigorous twining stemmed climber has attractive grey-green foliage and bright orange and yellow flowers on red stems in summer. More delicate is the smaller *T. tricolorum*; whose slender 60–90cm/2–3ft long stems are covered in tiny leaves, and in early summer in miniature red and yellow spur-red flowers. Remove dead material when the plants start to go dormant in winter, and keep the plant fairly dry until the tubers sprout again in spring.

Vines [C] Vines like *Parthenocissus* and *Vitis* do not like humidity, and don't do very well in a mixed conservatory. They are best treated as a special case and selected on the advice of a specialist supplier.

Wattakaka sinensis Fragrant white flowers with red spots in summer. Leaves are grey felted beneath.

FLOWERS FOR COOL CONSERVATORIES

Even the unheated conservatory can offer an interesting selection of exotic-looking flowering plants to add highlights of colour to your foliage groups. *See also* climbers (pages 110–113), many of which have fabulous blooms.

Acacia dealbata (Mimosa) 6m/20ft. The feathery foliage is an attractive grey-green colour and the familiar fluffy, bright yellow scented flowers are a welcome sight in winter. A vigorous grower.

Begonia pendula 20–25cm/8–10in. A good plant for hanging baskets with its large, brightly coloured blooms. It needs to be slightly shaded and sprayed regularly to keep the moss moist.

Camellia 2m/6ft. Glossy low-growing evergreen shrub which produces a mass of glorious single or double blooms of pink, red or white.

Callistemon (Bottle Brush) 1m/3ft. Vigorous evergreen shrub with fine feathery green leaves and brilliant red 'bottle brush' flowers. *C. speciosus* might grow to 2m/6ft and has a large 13cm/5in flower spike.

Fig 112 The Sensitive Plant, Mimosa pudica.

Carpenteria californica 1.8m/6ft. A bushy evergreen shrub with glossy dark green leaves against which the sparkling white flowers with gold stems really stand out in summer. Flowers are scented.

Datura x candida (Angel's Trumpet) A vigorous but poisonous shrub with large furry leaves and enormous bell-like white flowers with a strong fragrance. Orange and mauve forms are also available.

Dicksonia antarctica (Tree Fern) 1.8m/6ft. Tree ferns are a classic feature of the Victorian-style conservatory, and can be relied upon to produce a dramatic, exotic effect. The plant makes a large clump of frilly green fronds, the stems covered with reddish hairs and scales. Eventually it makes a dark, scaly tree-like trunk with the fronds on top – hence its common name. The stems should be kept constantly moist to prevent the roots, which travel down, from drying out. Shade is important, so protect the fern from direct sun.

Drejerella (Shrimp Plant) 15–30cm/6–12in. This plant gets its name from the strange shrimp-coloured flower bracts. These cover the plant on leggy stems of delicate leaves.

Erica gracilis 45cm/18in. A shrubby heather which produces clusters of pink and white bells in autumn and winter if given plenty of light and ventilation. Must have a lime-free compost.

Erythrina cristagalli (Cockspur-Coral Tree) 1.5m/5ft. Exotic Brazilian plant with glossy green leaves on spiny stems, and brilliant waxy red blossoms like tongues of fire in summer. Pruning back to within 15cm/6in of the base in late winter/early spring produces plenty of new flowering shoots. Keep dry in winter but feed and water regularly during the growing season.

Hibiscus 240cm/8ft. An evergreen shrub with a wide choice of huge, showy flowers that bloom throughout the summer. Prune by one-third in late winter.

Lantana camara 90cm/35in. Vigorous plant, producing clusters of tiny flowers turning from yellow on opening to deep red as they age. Cut back in winter and keep to 90cm/3ft to prevent it becoming leggy. Also available with white and pink flowers.

Leptospermum (New Zealand Tea Tree) 3–5m/10–16ft. Small leaved bush with masses of pretty pink-red flowers with black centres, according to type.

Luculia gratissima Will grow to the size of a small tree smothered in highly scented pink flowers in winter. Prune to shape in winter.

Oleander 3m/9ft. Large evergreen bush with straight stems of dark grey-green poisonous foliage. Red, pink or white flowers are supported in attractive clusters.

Pelargonium (Geranium) 23–60cm/9–24in. Geraniums and pelargoniums are easy to grow, and are hardy, preferring drought to humid heat, and providing a fine display in full sun and with little water for most of the year. There are a great many types, from dwarf forms and ramblers to variegated and scented types. Both foliage and flowers are attractive, the choice varying from zonal geraniums with special leaf markings to double-flowered pelargoniums. There are also some fifty varieties of scented-leaf geranium, offering a choice of fragrance ranging from rose and mint to lemon and spice.

Pittosporum tobira 'Variegatum' 1.2m/4ft. An evergreen shrub with grey-green leaves edged with cream. The white flowers smell strongly of orange blossom.

Sparmannia africana 1.2–2m/4–6ft. Grows to a handsome tree with large, slightly translucent pale green leaves and white flowers in summer. Prune back in winter to encourage it to grow bushy.

FLOWERS FOR HEATED CONSERVATORIES

If you can maintain a certain temperature in the heated conservatory during the day, and more importantly only a drop of several degrees at night, you can grow an exciting variety of tropical and sub-tropical plants. Many produce exotic blooms to liven up your collection and maybe release a bewitching scent. Ideally choose something of interest during summer and winter to enjoy the conservatory fully. Temperature will rely on the range of plants chosen – obviously it makes sense to select those with similar requirements. Also, if the room is to be used as a sitting

room or dining room, temperature and humidity will have to be comfortable for human inhabitants too. Plants with particular needs such as orchids and cacti must be treated as a special case (*see* pages 119–127).

Cassia corymbosa An evergreen shrub with delicate frondy foliage, producing sprays of golden yellow flowers. It is easy to grow, even from seed, and should be pruned back hard in spring if it grows too large.

Catharanthus roseus (Madagascar Periwinkle) 15cm/6in. This evergreen with small, glossy oval leaves and pink flowers is usually grown as an annual in the conservatory.

Crossandra infundibuliformis 'Mona Wallhead' 30cm–1m/1–3ft. Broad leaves set off the clusters of pretty orange flowers.

Cycads 1m/3ft. Strange-looking exotics, their palmy foliage like a primitive feathery head-dress. They produce a rosette of tough green fronds from a woody base made up of old dead leaves. These are slow-growing plants; most popular is *C. revoluta*, the Japanese Sago Palm, whose leathery fronds can reach 75cm/2.5ft from the cone-like base, after many years' growth.

Datura cornigera (Angel's Trumpet) 1.8m/6ft. A fast-growing shrub which can be trained as a standard. It has large, soft leaves and unusual hanging trumpet flowers in summer. The flowers are yellow and scented; a double form is 'Knightii'.

Datura sanguinea 1.8m/6ft. Flowers have no fragrance but are an attractive orange-red colour.

Dipladenia boliviensis 4.5m/15ft. An evergreen shrub producing clusters of white flowers with bright orange centres. Mature plants will twine and can be grown up canes. *Dipladenia* requires a humid atmosphere during the growing season.

115

Gardenia 30cm–2m/1–6ft. This is a plant that needs spraying frequently and must be kept warm in winter. But it is well worth the extra care, for it makes a lovely shrub with glossy dark green leaves and scented white flowers.

Guzmania 30–38cm/12–15in. A Bromeliad which makes a dense clump of green leaves with red tints from a central rosette. *G. lingulata* produces a red and yellow central flower spike; *G. monostachya* has a red and white flower stem 38cm/15in tall. This is a plant that likes heat but prefers a shady position.

Heliotropium arborescens (Cherry Pie) 30cm–1.2m/1–4ft. Popular for its mass of tiny violet flowers with a strong cherry-like fragrance.

Hibiscus (Rose Mallow) 2m/6ft. Makes a succession of large trumpet-like flowers in shades of

Fig 113 Guzmania dissitflora.

orange, pink or red against small, toothed green leaves. Needs plenty of water in summer.

Ixora coccinea (Flame of the Woods) 1m/3ft. An evergreen with shiny leaves and large clusters of red or pink flowers on red stems. Prefers a humid atmosphere.

Pentas lanceolata (Egyptian Star Cluster) 60cm/2ft. A winter-flowering shrub with hairy leaves and ball-like clusters of star-shaped pink flowers. Pinch out new shoots to keep a good shape.

Smithiantha cinnabarina (Temple Bells) 60–90cm/2–3ft. Thick velvety leaves and pink and yellow spotted flowers like drooping clusters of bells are the distinguishing features.

SHOWY BULBS

It is lovely to plant up narcissi and tulips, species crocus, hyacinths, polyanthus and primulas in pots and containers to bring into the conservatory just before they flower for a special seasonal display. But also consider planting a few of the more showy, exotic bulbs for an eye-catching talking point.

Agapanthus africanus 60–120cm/2–4ft. Large clusters of blue or white flowers against strap-like leaves.

Freesia refracta 50cm/18in. Delicate butterfly-like blooms with a strong, sweet scent and fresh colours from white, yellow and gold to pink, red and purple. Keep cool until growth starts and then introduce warmth gradually.

Haemanthus katharinae 30cm/12in. Produces large heads of spiky pink flowers in spring.

Hippeastrum 60–90cm/2–3ft. Popular for its dramatic trumpet-like blooms in white, pink or red on top of a very tall stem.

Fig 114 Bright golden primula have been used here to add a touch of spring cheer to a display of strongly contrasted foliage shapes.

Lilium auratum 60cm/2ft. The lily flowers are huge and white with red and gold streaks.

Lilium candidum (Madonna Lily) 60cm/2ft. Beautiful clustered stems of white lilies with gold centres.

Lilium tigrinum (Tiger Lily) 60cm/2ft. Lily blooms are speckled golden.

Sprekelia formosissima (Jacobean Lily) 30cm/ 12in. Produces a single or pair of large red flowers like orchids, as big as 13cm/5in across.

Vallota speciosa (Scarborough Lily) 60cm/2ft. In late summer a mass of bright red trumpet-shaped flowers come into bloom.

Zantedeschia aethiopica (Trumpet or Arum Lily) 90cm/3ft. A striking plant with arrow-shaped leaves and large white trumpet flowers in spring. *Z. elliottiana* has yellow flowers; those of *Z. rehmannii* are almost black.

INDOOR WATER PLANTS

A conservatory pool is a good idea if you have the space, since it helps improve humidity. Pool plants will also complement your conservatory species since they tend to be dramatic or exotic in appearance.

Colocasia esculenta 'Antiquorum' 45cm/18in. A marginal plant with large green leaves which have a purple tinge, and yellow arum-like flowers.

Cyperus alternifolius (Umbrella Plant) 1m/ 3ft. The tender, highly attractive Umbrella Plant is perfect for the pool side. It makes a clump of tall graceful stems with a cluster of spiky leaves on the top. It grows well in pots to a height of around 60cm/2ft.

Cyperus papyrus (Egyptian Paper Rush) 2–2.5m/6–8ft. Dramatic plant with large grassy heads on top of tall stems.

Eichhornia crassipes (Water Hyacinth) An attractive floating plant which makes a mass of blue and gold flowers.

Nymphaea (Water Lily) If you have a pool you must have water lilies and there are several that will do well indoors and look quite charming. *Nymphaea capensis* is one, also *N. stellata* and the night-flowering *N. lotus*. *Nelumbo nucifera* has large, round leaves and big pink or white blooms.

FRUIT AND VEGETABLES

The conservatory offers a good chance to grow more tender, perhaps decorative edible plants. Plant miniature hybrids in tubs and containers or hanging baskets to avoid it looking like a greenhouse. Extra care will be required with control of heat, humidity and ventilation to keep pests and diseases at bay if you wish to have good results.

117

Aubergine 'Bonica' is an F^1 hybrid with a compact, bushy habit. It produces plenty of large, shiny purple fruits. More unusual is 'Easter Egg', a novelty, all-white aubergine with a good flavour, each about 10cm/4in long and 5cm/2in across.

Citrus Oranges and lemons will thrive as a small evergreen shrub or small tree, flowering and bearing fruit if given plenty of light and a cool winter temperature of 4°C (39°F). The leaves, flowers and fruits are all highly attractive.

Courgettes Grow a high-yield variety like 'Ambassador F^1' and pick them while still tiny. 'Gold Rush' is unusual in that the slim fruits are a shining golden yellow.

Fig A fig will grow well indoors, especially against a rear wall and enjoying maximum exposure to sunlight. Roots usually prefer to be restrained within a pot or container.

Grapevine A single vine can be pruned to fit and will thrive, providing the conservatory is unheated – heat seems to encourage infestation with red spider mite. However, if you wish to grow tender flowering plants as well, choose a long season grape such as Muscat of Alexandria which can use the heat given to encourage ripening.

Melon Requires dry heat for a good flavour and plants should not be shaded, to encourage quick growth. Good ventilation essential. Choose your favourite shape and flavour – salmon-pink fleshed 'Sweetheart' or fragrant 'Ogen'.

Peach, Nectarine and Apricot Layer against a wall or grow in pots or small tubs. Choose heavy yield, compact varieties such as nectarine 'Humboldt', peach 'Duke of York', or apricot 'Hemskirk'.

Fig 115 Ficus benjamina *'Golden King'.*

Fig 116 Ficus diversifolia.

Strawberry Strawberries can be grown in special tubs or hanging baskets without fear of raids from slugs or birds. The plants themselves are attractive, with their tiny white flowers and bright red fruits. You can choose your favourite flavour without worrying if it is hardy enough.

Sweet Pepper An ornamental plant. Fruits will ripen more easily in a conservatory providing you can maintain a humid atmosphere. As well as the familiar red and green peppers. 'Wax Lights' ripen to yellow, white, red or violet; 'Yellow Lantern' is a golden yellow pepper. 'Redskin' has been specially developed for tubs and pots and makes a dwarf plant weighed down with glossy fruits.

Tomato Choose decorative small cherry-fruited varieties for tubs and hanging baskets in the conservatory. Plants will need to be well sprayed and watered and will not thrive in too hot an environment.

ORCHIDS

Despite their fantastic, exotic appearance, most orchids are surprisingly easy to grow, given the right conditions. If you are considering making a collection it is worth planning light, shading, heat and humidity before you buy your plants. Pro-pagation is equally simple, even for beginners, making it possible to build up stocks and ex-change plants with other enthusiasts, which will keep down the cost of a large collection. You will find the majority of species fall into three distinct temperature groups: cool (around 10°C/50°F); warm (18–21°C/65–75°F) and moderate (13°C/55°F). Obviously, collecting plants from one group only will make care and maintenance easier. Groups are indicated by: [C] cool; [M] moderate; [W] warm.

Ada aurantiaca [C] Grown for its brilliant orange flowers on compact sprays during the winter and spring. The individual blooms are small and not fully opening, producing a bell-shaped flower. This orchid can easily be raised from seed.

Aerides fieldingii [M–W] (Foxtail Orchid) A free-flowering species with drooping spikes often up to 60cm/24in long. The flowers in spring or summer are pinky-white and mottled with mauve, and sweet-scented. The plant is epiphytic and makes many aerial roots, so it needs a high degree of humidity; you therefore need to spray the plant frequently during the summer months.

Angraecum eburneum [W] This winter-flowering species produces 9–12 flowers with green sepals, petals and spur and a pure white lip. It should be watered throughout the year and sprayed overhead during the summer. Good light is needed but the plant should not be in bright sunlight for any length of time. An ideal position is in a hanging basket near to the glass – which should be shaded in summer.

Angraecum sesquipedale [W] 90cm/36in. Majestic star-shaped flowers in the winter that are cream-white in colour and have a long, greenish spur (30cm/12in). They are long-lasting and fragrant. The plant requires moist conditions and plenty of light but should be protected from full sun.

Anguloa clowesii [C] (Cradle or Tulip Orchid) The flowers in early summer are 7.5cm/3in across and are a bright canary yellow. This plant needs plenty of water and feed in the growing season. Water should be withheld when the leaves are shed at the end of the growing season.

Angulocaste 'Olympus' [C] Can become extremely large, so allow sufficient room. Grow in good light, with full light during the winter when it is dormant. The flowers come in spring with varying colours from white and cream to yellow. Do not spray overhead as this will damage the foliage.

Bifrenaria harrisoniae [C] Creamy-white flowers with thick waxy sepals and petals and a lip covered with red-purple hairs appear in early summer. The plant will thrive in a pot or hanging basket and should be kept drier at the root when not in active growth. Good drainage is important.

Brassia verrucosa [C] (Spider Orchid) The sweetly scented flowers are on sprays of up to a dozen blooms during early summer. They are light green with darker green spotting. A good plant to mount on wood when long aerial roots are produced.

Brassolaeliocattleya 'Crusader' [M] This hybrid has large pink flowers in winter. They have a heavy purple round lip and a yellow patch inside the lobes. It needs very good light and a rest after flowering. During the rest don't let the pseudobulbs shrivel too much.

Brassolaeliocattleya Norman Bay 'Lows' [M] A rose-magenta flowered hybrid with flowers 20cm/8in across. They have a splendid frilled lip and scent. Should be grown in good light and rested for part of the year after flowering.

Bulbophyllum collettii [M] Maroon-red flowers with yellow stripes in spring, this orchid is not deeply rooted so requires a shallow pot or attachment to a tree fern or cork bark. Good drainage is essential.

Calanthe vestita [W] This easy grower is ideal for the warm conservatory. The flowers range in colour from white to dark pink with the lip often stronger in colour than the rest of the flower. Water well and feed during the growing season and until the leaves fall during early winter.

Cattleya aurantiaca [C] A small bifoliate species with drooping clusters of red-orange blooms in summer.

Cattleya Bow Bells [M] Pure white flowers 15cm/6in across with overlapping petals and a sulphur-yellow mark in the back of the throat are the distinguishing features of this hybrid. To encourage these blooms to last longer the plants should be kept dry while in flower.

Cattleya bowringiana [M] An autumn-flowering species with rose-purple blooms, deep purple lip and a golden yellow mark in the throat. Withhold watering during its winter rest after flowering. Keep in a well-drained compost.

Cattleya forbesii [M] Yellow or tan-coloured flowers in late summer that have a tubular lip with side lobes of pale pink on the outside and a deep yellow throat marked with wavy red lines. Do not over-pot but keep in as small a pot as possible. It needs good light all year round and lightly spraying in the summer.

Coelogyne ochracea [C] Pretty flowers full of fragrance in early summer. Flowers and growth will finish in autumn when the plant will rest. Place in full light in winter and do not water until the new growths appear in early spring.

Cymbidium angelic 'Advent' [C] This hybrid has yellow flowers in autumn and winter. The petals and sepals are a pale yellow and the cream-coloured lip is spotted with dark red. Spray during the summer months when the plant should be kept cool at night.

Cymbidium Ayres Rock 'Cooksbridge Velvet' [C] Large flowers in winter and spring are crimson, tinged with white, and the lip is dark crimson edged with white. A supporting cane is needed for the heavy flower spikes and it is best to cut the spike after the last flower has been open for about ten days, as this will reduce strain on the plant. The spike will last a long time in water in a cool room.

Cymbidium Bulbarrow 'Our Midge' [C] This Bulbarrow hybrid has rose-red flowers in late spring with deep crimson lips. Can be prone to red spider mite, so sponge and wipe the leaves regularly with water.

Cymbidium devonianum [C] This miniature species has flowers in spring. They are green speckled with red and the lip is clouded with purple. Needs a semi-rest in winter with only occasional watering.

Cymbidium Dingwall 'Lewes' [C] Free-flowering hybrid with white sepals and petals and a lip marked with red. Keep plant well shaded when flowering.

Cymbidium Fort George 'Lewes' [C] Very fine green-flowering hybrid with up to fourteen flowers per spike. To keep the plant flowering well, repot every other year. You can also grow these plants in large beds.

Cymbidium lowianum [C] This plant flowers in late spring, producing large arching sprays of green flowers with a V-shaped red mark on the lip.

Cymbidium Peter Pan 'Greensleeves' [C] This popular autumn-flowering variety will grow easily in a conservatory and has a compact habit. Petals and sepals are soft green and the lip is marked and edged with deep crimson. Don't keep the plants on the stem for more than a couple of weeks. Cut them and place in a vase of water.

Cymbidium Stonehaven 'Cooksbridge' [C] Medium-sized plant with strong spikes, the flowers open in autumn and are cream-coloured with a pale yellow lip edged with dark red. Spikes need supporting by cane.

Cymbidium Touchstone 'Janis' [C] This miniature hybrid produces arching sprays of bronze flowers with crimson lips in winter. Keep watered throughout the year. Cool night time temperature is important.

Cymbidium traceyanum [C] Autumn to winter flowering with long arching sprays of flowers. The flowers are strongly scented, but not too pleasantly. The petals are green, striped dark red, the white lip is spotted red.

Dendrobium aureum [C] In winter, this is a deciduous orchid, when it needs a rest from watering and a good light position. Flowers in early spring are creamy-yellow with a buff brown lip, and are fragrant. Watch out for red spider mite during the growing season and repot after flowering.

Dendrobium densiflorum [C] 5cm/2in flowers are carried in trusses from nodes at the top of the club-shaped bulbs. They develop quickly in spring and last for up to ten days. The colour is golden yellow. Keep dry while in flower and in full light during autumn and winter.

Dendrobium 'Fiftieth State' [W] This plant succeeds in high temperatures and almost full sunlight. Water it freely while growing but rest it after flowering. Flowers are long-lasting and a magenta colour.

Dendrobium nobile [C] Flowers appear in ones and twos during spring. They are rosy purple at the tip, shading to white at the centre. The lip has a maroon blotch in the throat. Withhold water during the winter rest, water well in summer.

Dendrobium pierardii [M] Needs full light during winter, when it is deciduous. Blooms in spring are pastel pink and the rounded lip is creamy yellow streaked with purple. Water after flowering, spray regularly during growing season to keep red spider mite at bay.

Dendrobium secundum [M] Unusual flowers that are clustered together into compact sprays. They are rosy pink with an orange blotch on the lips and appear for a long period during spring and summer.

121

Dendrobium transparens [M] Free-flowering species that grows well on bark in a pendant position. It flowers early, producing pale mauve blooms. It is deciduous and should not be watered during its rest period.

Dendrobium wardianum [C] White flowers with petal, sepals and lip tipped with purple appear in winter. The lip is also stained yellow with two maroon blotches at the base. Watch out for red spider and water well during the growing season. Provide good winter light.

Encyclia vitellina [C] Fairly tolerant of drier conditions so is good for conservatories. Star-shaped flowers of orange-red appear in autumn. Can be grown in a pot or on a piece of cork bark. Needs a dry rest in winter.

Epidendrum ibaguense [C] A reed-stem species that produces rounded leaves and many aerial roots. Flowers are orange, red or scarlet. This plant needs good light.

Epidendrum stamfordianum [M] Many-flowered spike with scented yellow blooms spot-ted red in early summer. Needs a good light posi-tion and plenty of water during the summer. Needs a complete winter rest.

Laelia anceps [C] An erect flower spike 60cm/2ft high and producing two to five flowers in autumn, which are pale or deep rose pink. It will flourish in a cool conservatory with good light and prefers to be grown on a block of wood or cork bark.

Laelia gouldiana [C–M] Winter-flowering epiphytic with brightly coloured cattleya-like flowers, which are rose-purple, and last several weeks. Needs good light to encourage flowering.

Laelia purpurata [M] The national flower of Brazil, with blooms 13–18cm/5–7in across that vary in colour from white to pale purple. Moderate light is required, as is good drainage.

Lycaste aromatica [C–M] Heavily scented bright yellow flowers from winter to spring. The plant needs warmth and moisture when in full growth, but cooler and drier conditions when at rest.

Lycaste cruenta [C–M] Fragrant large flowers of beautiful yellow-green sepals and deep golden petals and lip. The throat is stained deep red. Needs high summer temperatures, but a cooler rest period. Leaves turn yellow and drop off in autumn.

Lycaste virginalis [C–M] This many-coloured orchid (white to deep pink) has flowers up to 15cm/6in across in winter and spring. It is easy to grow in a conservatory but does not like to be over-wet at any time and must be kept dry in winter.

Maclellanara 'Pagan Lovesong' [C–M] Vigorous and robust growing hybrid that can be grown in almost any climate. The blooms are yellow-green with large occasional dark brown spots. The lip is white, and is also spotted dark brown. This plant grows all year and should be well watered and fed throughout the year.

Maxillaria picta [C] Pretty flowers produced prolifically on single stems. They are yellow on the inside with red-brown bars on the outside. They appear in the winter and have a strong fragrance. Keep moist in the summer.

Maxillaria porphyrostele [C–M] Will grow in little space in a hanging basket. Plants produce a number of short flower spikes which carry a yellow flower that is long-lasting in winter and spring. Grow in good light and spray during summer.

Odontoglossum bictoniense [C] Erect flower spikes at the end of summer. The flowers open in succession so that there are often eight or nine out at once. These are yellow-green with brown spots and a white or pink lip. Needs

122

medium shade but no resting in winter, though reduce water after flowering has finished.

Odontoglossum cervantesii [C] A dwarf form that is only 15cm/6in high – ideal for those with limited space. The flowers in winter and early spring are white and marked with chestnut rings. Do not let it dry out during the growing season. Reduce water during winter and provide medium shade in the summer.

Odontoglossum grande (Clown Orchid) [C] The chestnut-brown markings in the centre of the yellow flower give this plant its common name. Needs plenty of moisture at the roots during the growing season but not high humidity, as this will damage the foliage.

Odontoglossum pulchellum (Lily of the Valley Orchid) [C] Waxy white flowers bloom in masses and have a fine scent. It flowers in the spring and needs medium shade in the summer. Will need supporting if you wish the flower spikes to stand erect.

Oncidium ornithorhynchum [C] Compact habit with light-green pseudobulbs. The short arching flower spikes are produced freely in the autumn and carry the flowers on side branches. These are lilac with a yellow crest on the lip, long lasting and fragrant. The plant dislikes cold and damp, so do not spray or keep too wet.

Oncidium tigrinum [C] Beautiful autumn-flowering species which has several fragrant flowers on each branch and the terminal part of the stem. Petals and sepals are yellow barred with brown and the lip is a vivid yellow.

Paphiopedilum callosum [M] Vigorous-growing species with long-lasting flowers. The flowers are 10cm/4in across and coloured varying shades of purple and green. Keep evenly moist throughout the year and don't expose to bright light.

Paphiopedilum Maudiae [M] One of the most popular *Paphiopedilum* hybrids in the world, with its mottled light and dark green foliage and single large bloom marked in white and apple green.

Paphiopedilum Miller's Daughter 'Snow Maiden' [M] Beautiful white flowers 13cm/5in across are the distinguishing feature of this hybrid. This flower is also speckled with pinkish-brown. The plant needs moist, shady conditions and should never be allowed to dry out completely; equally, it doesn't like being overwatered.

Paphiopedilum Royale 'Downland' [M] Easy to grow providing conditions are warm and shady. Winter flowers are soft rose-red with green shading and are heavy enough to need supporting. The blooms last for up to ten weeks, when the stems should be cut for new growth.

Phalaenopsis lueddemanniana [W] A free-flowering evergreen producing several flower spikes at the same time with as many as twenty 2.5cm/1in flowers in spring and summer. White or yellow petals are marked with pink or purple spots and the small lip is purple. It likes warm shade, but cooler, shadier conditions will produce deeper colours. There are some interesting hybrid forms.

Phalaenopsis schllerana [W] A beautiful plant with silver marbled deep green leaves up to 46cm/18in long and arching spikes of pretty mauve flowers 5–7.5cm/2–3in across. Visible roots are equally attractive. Many good hybrids.

Phalaenopsis 'Temple Cloud' [W] Beautiful white blooms for months at a time providing warm shade is supplied. Grow in as small a pot as possible and do not allow to dry out.

Pleione formosana var. alba 'Snow White' [C] Pure white single flowers with lightly spotted lip. Will tolerate very cool conditions. Store over winter in a cool, dry place.

Ryhnchostylis retusa [M]   Densely flowered spike produces the familiar 'foxtail' bloom. The flowers themselves are waxy white and heavily scented, with magenta markings. Flowers from winter to spring.

Stanhopea tigrina [C–M]   Short-lived but beautiful flowers are highly scented in ivory with maroon-purple blotches. The flower spike grows downwards so the plant must be grown in a special wire or wooden slatted basket.

Stanhopea wardii [C–M]   Flowers in late summer with yellow or orange blooms and brown purple markings. Easy to grow in purpose-made baskets so that the exotic-shaped flowers can bloom from below.

Vanda cristata [C–M]   A small orchid, only about 25cm/10in tall. The yellow-green flowers are waxy and fragrant, with blood-red stripes and spots. Free-flowering from spring to summer in good light.

Vuyistekeara Cambria 'Plush' [C–W]   Easy to grow in any environment, producing a stem of large glowing red flowers with big red and white lips.

Wilsonara 'Widecombe Fairy' [C–M] Tolerant of temperature changes, this is an easy-to-grow orchid providing it is kept moist all year. The tiny star-shaped white flowers with pink markings look stunning displayed along the large branches.

CACTI

With their strange, almost extra-terrestrial appearance, cacti have a fascination and appeal that makes them ideal for making up a specialist collection. They look best arranged in groups, on trays, shelves or in shallow troughs where their huge variety in shape and size can best be displayed. Spines and hairs, globe, pebble and columnar shapes provide plenty of contrasts, and most will produce curious flowers too, many of them scented.

Aporocactus   1m/3ft. A trailing plant with long stems, producing some easy-to-grow cultivars including *A. flagellaformis*, the Rat's Tail Cactus, which has slender stems and bright crimson zygomorphic flowers. Needs light, but not full sun. *A. mallisonii* is free-flowering with deep scarlet flowers.

Ariocarpus   Low growing and spineless, this cactus is sometimes called 'Living Rock'. Likes full sun. *A. fissuratus* makes grey, warty tubercles to around 20cm/8in diameter. Central flowers are purplish-pink. *A. retusus* has white flowers.

Astrophytum   10cm/4in. A wide variety of forms within this genus, some of which are spineless. *A. asterias*, the Bishop's Mitre, looks like a spineless sea urchin and has yellow flowers. *A. capricorne* has long twisted black spines; *A. ornatum* also has spines and green, white or grey body colour. Bishop's Cap, *A. myriostigma*, is round with white woolly scales and yellow flowers.

Cephalocereus   6m/18ft. A tall columnar cactus requiring complete dryness in winter. *C. senilis*, Old Man Cactus, is covered in long white hairs and produces pink flowers about 5cm/2in long.

Cereus   1m/3ft. Elegant and easy to grow, flowers are mostly scented and bloom at night. *C. peruvianus* has dark green stems with brown-black spines and large white flowers.

Coryphantha   A genus of globular plants with stiff spines requiring full sunlight, usually flowering from the crown. *C. clava* is a blue-green colour with yellow or brown spines and large yellow

Fig 117 (Opposite)   Phalaenopsis *orchid.*

flowers with green and red markings. *C. palmeri* has yellow flowers with brown stripes and woolly areoles on young plants.

Disocactus Strap-like leaves and white to scarlet flowers in winter. Needs heat. *D. macranthus* flowers easily early in the year with fragrant cream blooms.

Echinocactus A large, barrel-shaped cactus, this plant is sometimes called the Hedgehog Cactus since it has lots of spines and only small flowers.

Echinocerus 20cm/8in. Usually make spiny low growing clumps with large colourful flowers that last well. There are a great many species, including *E. blanckii* which is semi-erect with large purplish-red flowers; and *E. knippelianus*, a globular cactus with woolly areoles and lots of pale magenta flowers in spring.

Espostoa Column-shaped, nocturnal flowering cacti which require full sun; many have long, white hairs in maturity like *E. lanata*, which has attractive yellow to red spines.

Ferocactus 13cm/5in. Large barrel-shaped plants with strong spines which may be straight or hooked. On *F. acanthodes* these are bright red and yellow; *F. viridescens* has red spines which fade to pink with age.

Gymnocalycium 3.3–28cm/2–14in. Smooth waxy body and bell-shaped flowers. Easy to grow if shaded in summer. *G. mihanovitchii* has a grey-green body with red markings and yellow flowers; *G. horstii* has a dark green glossy body and peach-pink flowers; the large *G. saglione* has red-brown curved spines and pinkish-white flowers

Heliocereus Climbing plant with stiff spines and beautiful flowers. A large, rich scarlet in *H. speciosus* or huge and lilac purple on *var. superbus*.

Hylocereus Climbing vine-like plants, easy to grow and nocturnal flowering. *H. undatus* will extend to many metres and produces large, fragrant white blooms. *H. purpusii* is blue-green with large white to golden yellow flowers.

Lemaireocereus Columnar and clump forming, these plants enjoy full sun. *L. thurberi* has large white flowers.

Mammillaria 10–20cm/4–8in. Some two hundred species are included in this genera and most are small growing. Flowers are also small but there are plenty of them and they last a long time. Plants need a rich soil and full sun, being allowed to dry out completely in winter. *M. elongata* has cylindrical stems and white, yellow or brown spines. *M. plumosa* is completely covered with white feathery spines. *M. spinosissima* grows to around 25cm/10in with yellow to brown spines and red flowers, while *M. zeilmanniana* has a dark green body and plenty of reddish-purple flowers.

Monvillea Erect or semi-erect plants with tall slender stems and attractive flowers. *M. cavendishii* has white flowers, about 12cm/5in long.

Notocactus A range of globular or columnar shapes, mostly free flowering. *N. ottonis* grows to around 10cm/4in in diameter and has reddish spines with shiny golden flowers; *N. leninghausii* is very attractive with large golden flowers on the flattened top of a columnar stem and a mass of golden spines as fine as hairs.

Nyctocereus Robust, erect plants enjoying high temperatures in summer but cool in winter. *N. sepentinus* becomes creeping and has scented white flowers at night.

Opuntia (Prickly Pear) A huge genus requiring plenty of sun and water in the growing season, and a complete rest period. There are a great many species including the blue-grey *O. gosseliniana* with bright yellow flowers or *O. microdasys*, the classic rabbit-ears shape with colourful areoles.

Pachycereus l2m/36ft. Large, tree-like plant with a short trunk. Young plants make good specimens for conservatories, but they require plenty of light. They would not grow too large for many years. *P. pringlei* is the best known and has many spines with handsome black tips.

Parodia 5–8cm/2–3in. Small round bodies with attractive spines and flowers. *P. chrysacanthion* is smothered in gold spines, producing woolly flower buds from the crown and deep yellow flowers. *F. sanguiniflora* has deep red flowers and a bright green body.

Pereskia A clambering plant with long slender stems and real leaves. If you can maintain a temperature not less than l0°C/50°F, you can grow free-flowering, tropical *P. aculeata* which produces dark green leaves and scented clusters of cream flowers.

Rebutia (var) A large group of small, globular plants, usually growing in clusters. A good conservatory plant, especially the tiny *R. minuscula* (2.5–4cm/l–1.5in), which has a glossy green body, short white spines and bright red flowers. Other species include orange, pink, white and purple flowered forms.

Schlumbergera (var) A popular group, including autumn and winter flowering types. Known as Zygocactus, but more commonly as the Christmas Cactus, *S. truncata*. Varieties and cultivars include white, magenta, orange and pink flowers.

Sulcorebutia Pronounced areoles and colourful flowers. Do not allow the temperature to fall below l0°C/50°F in winter. *S. steinbachii* is small, dark green and globular with dark red flowers. *S. menesesii* has pink spines and yellow flowers.

Tacinga A type of prickly pear, tall and easy to grow. *T. funalis* has grey-blue branches with greenish-white flowers at the tips.

Thelocactus 20cm/8in. Colourful sun-lovers including *T. iopothele* which has pale yellow flowers and *T. bicolor* with red, brown and yellow spines, up to 2.5cm/lin long, and purple-pink flowers 6cm/2in long.

Wilcoxia Long slender stems and colourful flowers. *W. poselgeri* is grey-green with tiny spines and purple-pink flowers.

Index